The Word Book

Elizabeth Stenson
Barbara Antheunis

I(T)P
International Thomson Publishing
The trademark ITP is used under license

Second Edition
© Nelson Canada,
A Division of Thomson Canada Limited, 1995
All rights reserved.

17-604714-X

Published in 1995 by
Nelson Canada

Illustrations by Margaret Kaufhold and Tracy Walker
Design by Julia Hall

Nelson Canada
An International Thomson Publishing Company

Toronto • New York • London • Bonn • Boston • Detroit • Madrid • Melbourne • Paris
Mexico City • Singapore • Tokyo • Albany NY • Belmont CA • Cincinatti OH

A a

about

above

accept

accident

acorn

across

act

activity, activities

add

address

adventure

afraid

after

afternoon

again

age

ago

ahead

accident

acorn

address

air

airplane

airport

alive

all

allowance

all right

almost

alone

along

alphabet

already

also

always

am

ambulance

an

and

angry

animal   (Look at pages 124 and 125.)

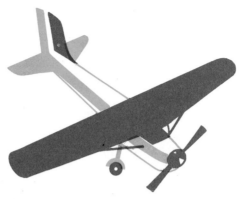

airplane

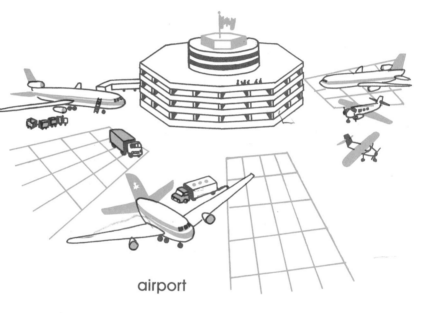

airport

ambulance

another

answer

ant

any

anybody

any more

anyone

anything

anywhere

apart

apartment

apple

aquarium

are

arena

aren't

arm

around

arrive, arriving, arrived

as

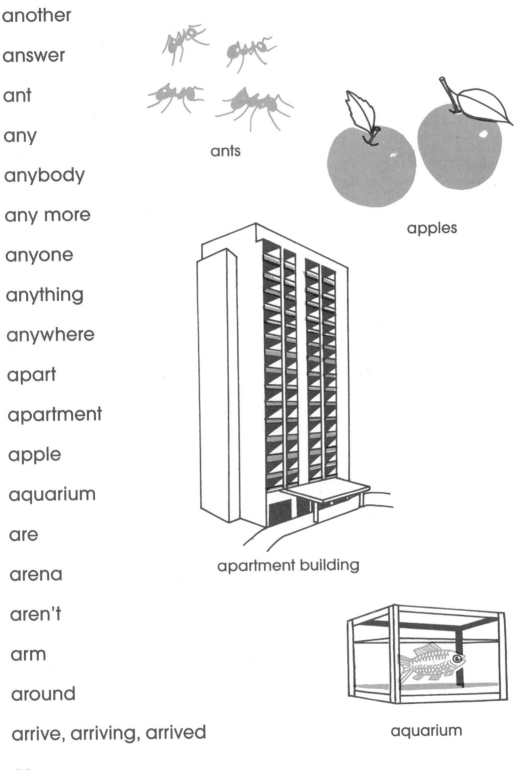

ants

apples

apartment building

aquarium

ask

asleep

astronaut

at

ate

attic

audio

aunt

autumn

awake

away

awful

awhile

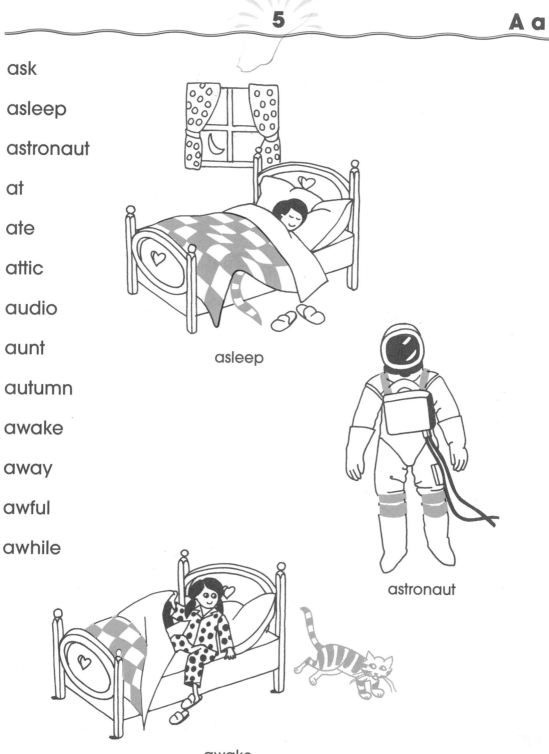

asleep

astronaut

awake

B b

baby, babies

back

backyard

bad

bag

bake, baking, baked

ball

ballet

balloon

banana

bang

bank

barbecue

bare

bark

barn

baseball   (Look at page 97.)

basement

baby

ballet

balloons

bananas

barbecue

basket

basketball

bat

bath

bathroom

be

beach

bean

beanstalk

bear

beard

beat

beautiful

beaver

because

bed

bedroom

bedtime

bee

been

basket

bat

bat

beaver

bees

beanstalk

beep

before

beg, begging, begged

begin, beginning, began, begun

behind

believe, believing, believed

bell

belong

below

belt

bench, benches

berry, berries

beside

best

bet

better

between

bicycle

big, bigger, biggest

bike

bell

belt

bench

bicycle
bike

big, bigger, biggest

bill

bird

birthday

bit

bite, biting, bit, bitten

blanket

blizzard

block

blond

blood

blow, blowing, blew, blown

boat

body, bodies　　(Look at page 98.)

bone, bony

book

boot

boring

borrow

boss, bossy

both

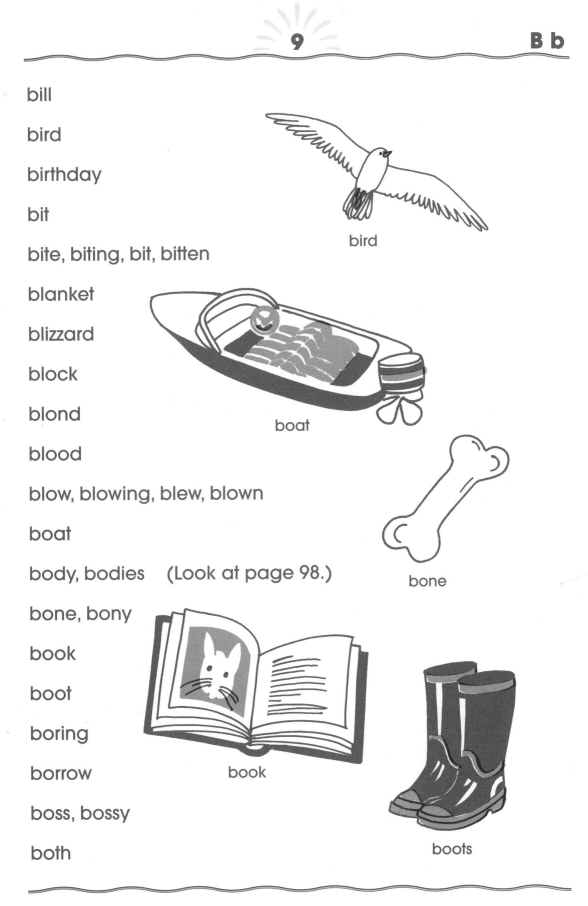

bird

boat

bone

book

boots

bottle

bottom

bought

bounce, bouncing, bounced

bow

bowl

box, boxes

boy

boyfriend

brain

branch, branches

brave

bread

break, breaking, broke, broken

breakfast

brick

bride

bridge

bright

bring, bringing, brought

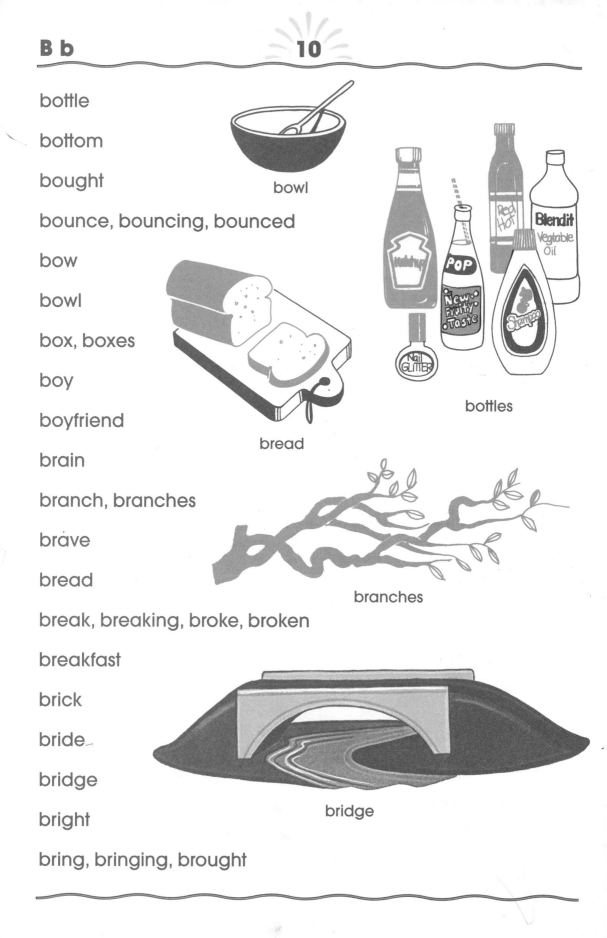

bowl

bread

bottles

branches

bridge

broke

broken

broom

brother

brought

Brownie

brush

bubble

bud

bug

build, building, built

bulldozer

bump

bunch, bunches

bunk

bunny, bunnies

burn

burst, bursting, burst

bury, burying, buried

bus, buses

bulldozer

Brownie

broom

bus

bush, bushes

busy

but

butcher

butter

butterfly, butterflies

button

buy, buying, bought

buzz

by

bye

butcher

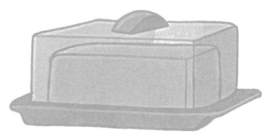

butter

buttons

butterflies

C c

cage

cake

calculator

calf, calves

call

camcorder

came

camera

camp

camper

can

Canada, Canadian

candy, candies

cannot

canoe

can't

car

card

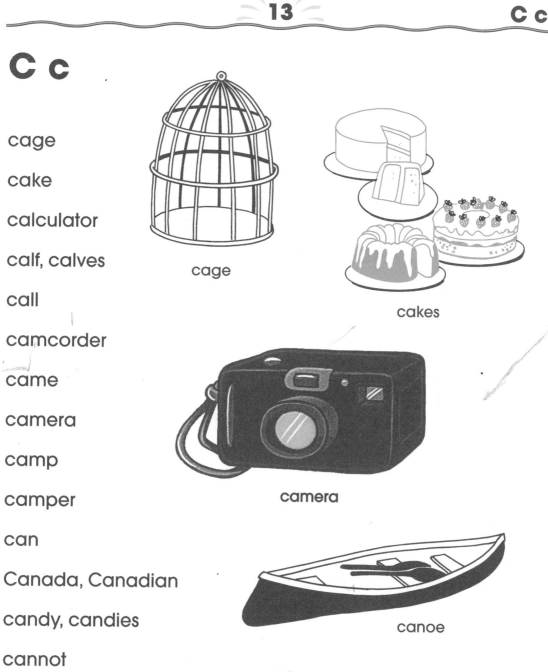

cage

cakes

camera

canoe

cards

care, carefully

carrot

carry, carrying, carried

cast

castle   (Look at page 99.)

cat

catch, catching, caught

caterpillar

cattle

celebration   (Look at pages 100 and 101.)

cent

centre, center

chair

change, changing, changed

chase, chasing, chased

cheat

check

cheek

cheese

cherry, cherries

carrot

caterpillars

cent

chair

cherries

chest

chesterfield

chew

chicken

chicken pox

chief

child, children

chin

chipmunk

chocolate

choose, choosing, chose, chosen

chop, chopping, chopped

church

circle

circus

city, cities

clap, clapping, clapped

class, classes

classroom

claw

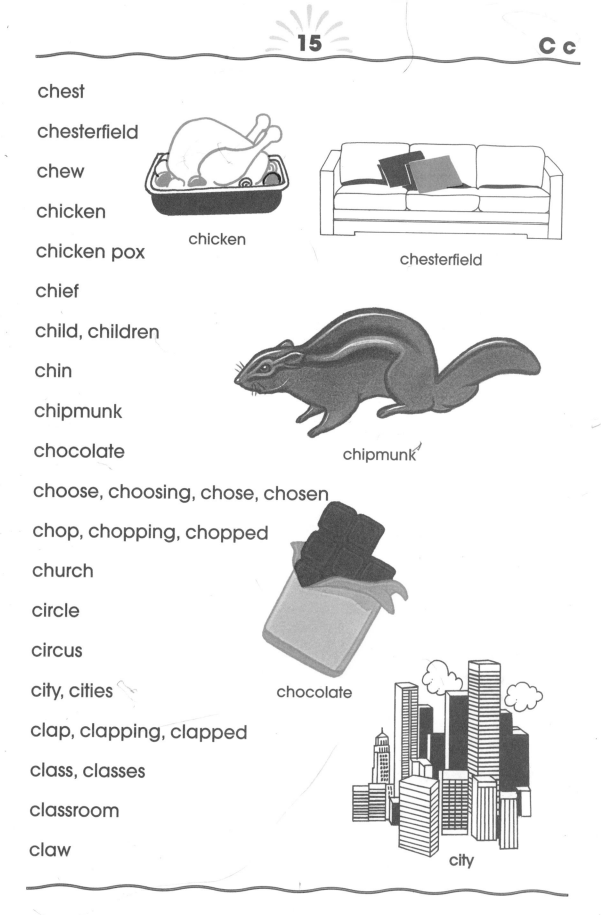

chicken

chesterfield

chipmunk

chocolate

city

clean

climb

clock

close, closing, closed

closet

clothes

cloud

clown

club

coach

coat

cold

collect

collection

colour, color

colt

comb

come, coming, came

comet

command

clock

colt

clown

comb

clothes

coat

hat

mitts

T-shirt

jeans

dress

socks

jacket

community, communities　(Look at page 102.)

compact disc

computer

contest

controls

cook

cookie

cool

corn

corner

cost

costume

cottage

couch

could

couldn't

count

counter

country, countries

courage

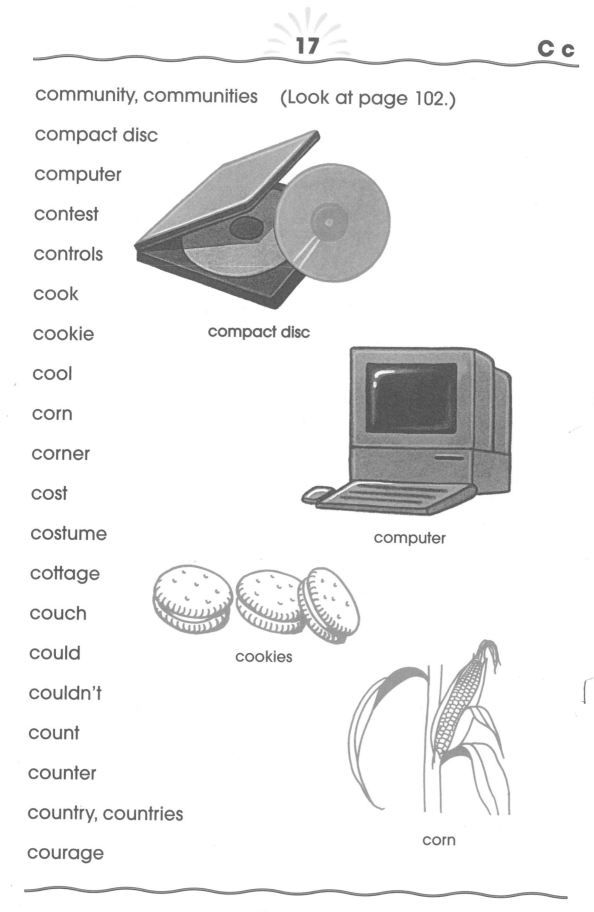

compact disc

computer

cookies

corn

cousin

cover

cow

cowboy

crack

crash

crawl

crayon

crazy

creature

creep, creeping, crept

crooked

cross

crowd

crown

cruel

crumb

crunch

cry, crying, cried

cub

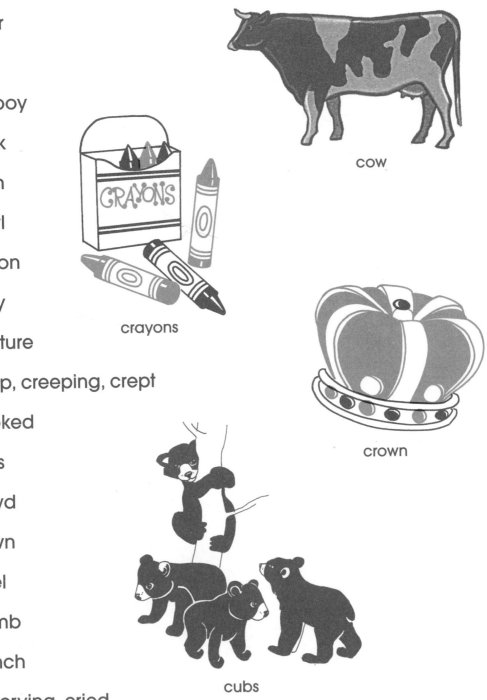

cow

crayons

crown

cubs

Cub

cup

cupboard

curious

curly

cut

cute

Cubs

cup

cut

D d

dad

daddy, daddies

dance, dancer

danger, dangerous

dare

dark

dancers

daughter

day

day-care

dead

dear

decide, deciding, decided

decorate, decoration

deep

deer

defence, defense

delicious

deliver

dentist

department

desert

desk

dessert

detective

devil

diamond

deer

dentist

desert

desk

dessert

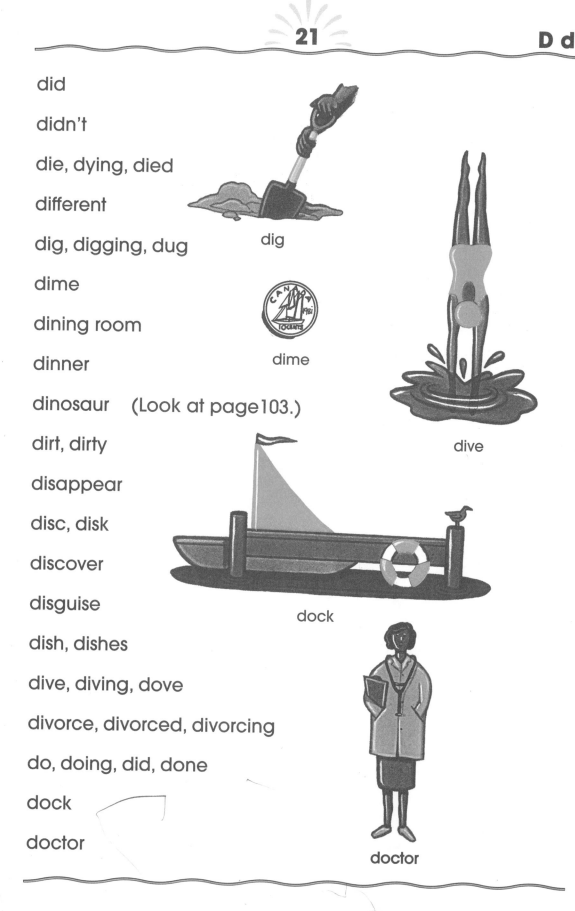

did

didn't

die, dying, died

different

dig, digging, dug

dig

dime

dining room

dime

dinner

dinosaur   (Look at page 103.)

dirt, dirty

dive

disappear

disc, disk

discover

disguise

dock

dish, dishes

dive, diving, dove

divorce, divorced, divorcing

do, doing, did, done

dock

doctor

doctor

does

doesn't

dog

doghouse

doll

dollar

dolphin

done

don't

door

doughnut

down

downstairs

downtown

drag, dragging, dragged

dragon

drank

draw, drawing, drew, drawn

dream

dress, dresses

dog

dolls

dolphin

doughnuts

dresses

drink, drinking, drank, drunk

drip, dripping, dripped

drive, driving, drove, driven

driver

driveway

drop, dropping, dropped

drum

dry

duck

dug

dumb

driveway

drums

duck

E e

each

ear

early, earlier, earliest

earth

east

easy

eat, eating, ate, eaten

edge

edit

egg

either

elephant

elevator

elf, elves

else

empty

end

enemy, enemies

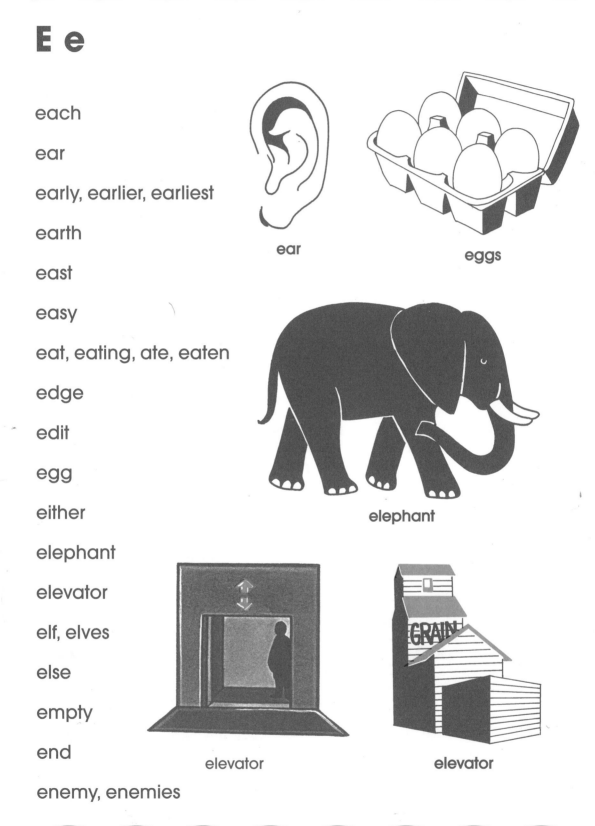

ear

eggs

elephant

elevator

elevator

engine

English

enjoy

enormous

enough

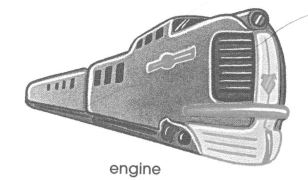

engine

environment　(Look at pages 104 and 105.)

equipment

escalator

escape, escaping, escaped

even

evening

ever

every

everybody

everyone

everything

everywhere

excellent

escalators

except

excite, exciting, excited

excuse

expensive

explore, exploring, explored

explosion

eye

eye

factory

F f

face

factory, factories

fair

fairground

fairy, fairies

fall

falling, fell, fallen

family, families   (Look at page106.)

fairground

famous

fantastic

far

farm   (Look at page 107.)

farther

fast

fasten

fat

father

favourite, favorite

fawn

feather

feed, feeding, fed

feel, feeling, felt

feet

fell

fence

ferry, ferries

few

field

fawn

feather

fence

ferry

fierce

fight, fighting, fought

fill

film

find, finding, found

fine

finger

finish

fire

firefighter

first

fish

fit

fix

flashlight

flat

flew

flip, flipping, flipped

float

floor

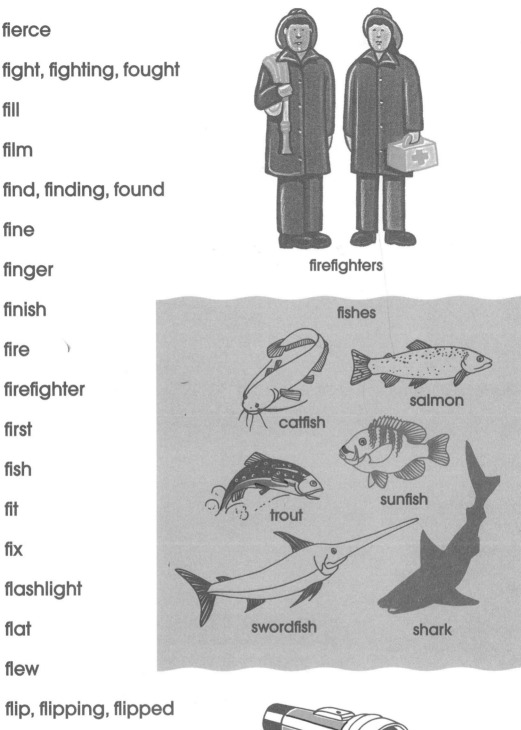

firefighters

fishes

catfish

salmon

trout

sunfish

swordfish

shark

flashlight

flour

flower

fluffy

fly, flies

fly, flying, flew, flown

follow

food

fool

foot, feet

football

footstep

for

forest

forget, forgetting, forgot, forgotten

fort

fortune

forward

fought

found

fountain

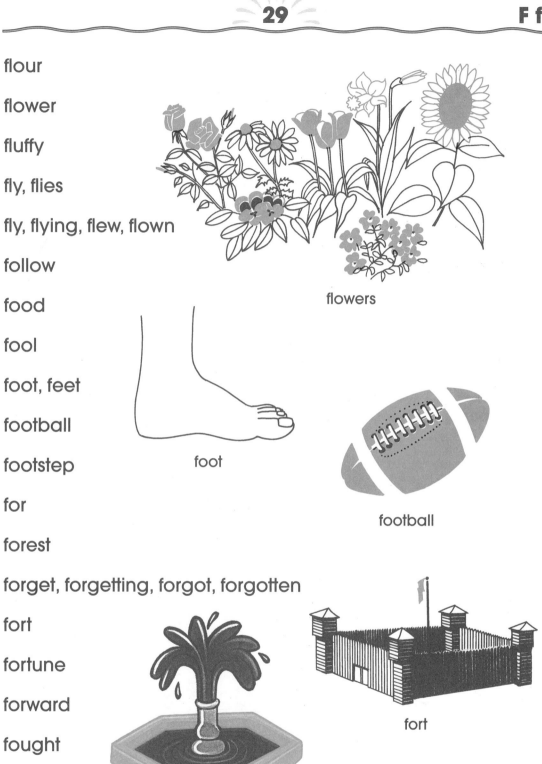

flowers

foot

football

fort

fountain

fox, foxes

fraction

free

freeze, freezing, froze, frozen

French

french fries

fresh

fridge

friend, friendly

frighten

frog

from

front

frost

frozen

fruit

fry, frying, fried

full

fun

funny, funnier, funniest

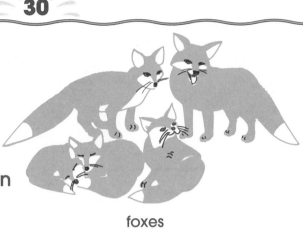

foxes

french fries

fridge

fruit

pear   grapes   cherries   apple

strawberries   lemon   pineapple

fur

furniture

furry

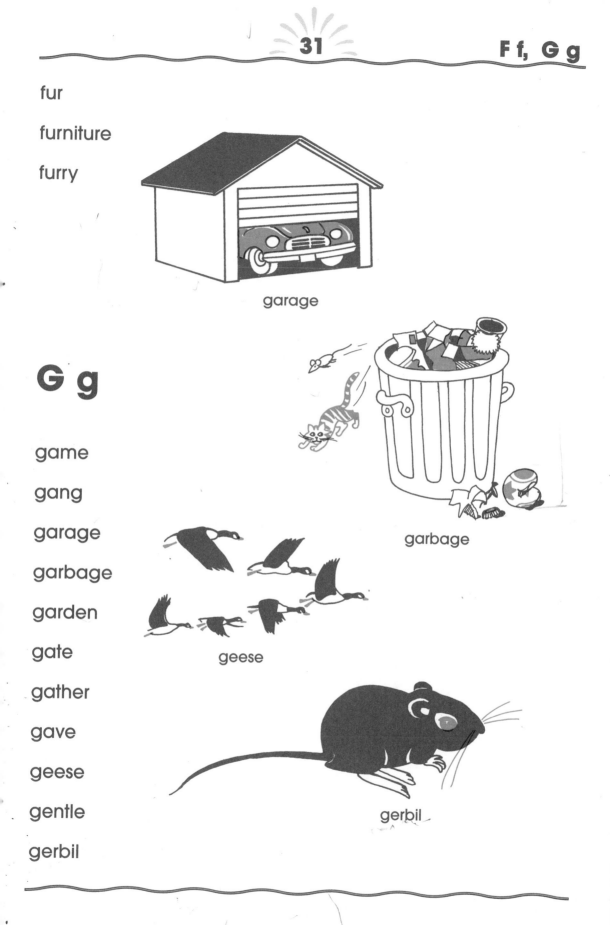

garage

G g

game

gang

garage

garbage

garden

gate

gather

gave

geese

gentle

gerbil

garbage

geese

gerbil

get, getting, got, gotten

ghost

giant

gift

giggle, giggling, giggled

giraffe

girl

girlfriend

gifts

give, giving, gave, given

glad

giraffe

glass, glasses

glove

glue

glasses

glasses

go, going, went, gone

goal, goalie

goat

gobble, gobbling, gobbled

God

goes

goat

gold, golden

goldfish

gone

good

goodbye

goose, geese

gorilla

got, gotten

grab, grabbing, grabbed

grade

grain

grandfather

grandmother

grandparents

grape

grass

grasshopper

great

greedy

grew

grocery, groceries

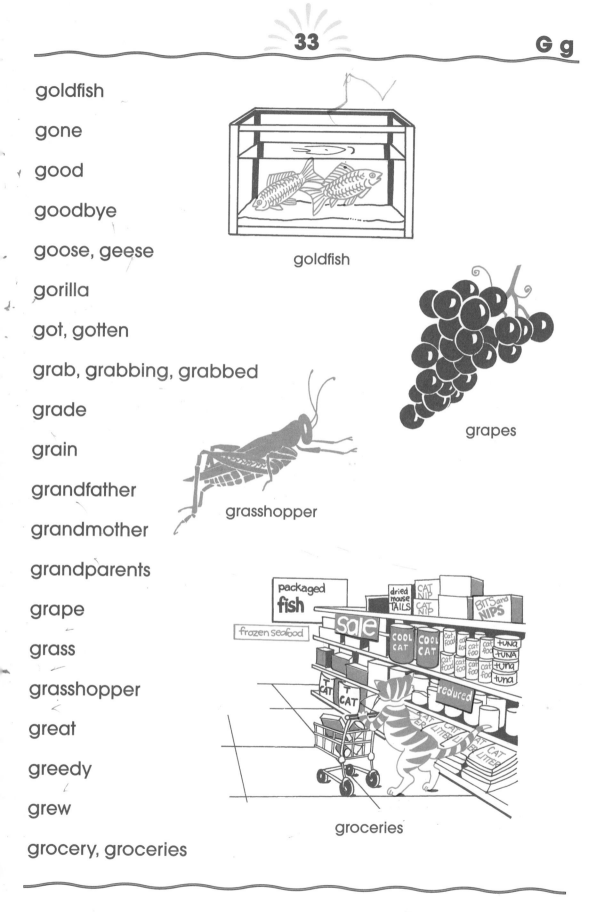

goldfish

grapes

grasshopper

groceries

ground

groundhog

group

grow, growing, grew, grown

growl

guard

guess

guest

guinea pig

guitar

gull

gum

gun

guppy, guppies

guy

gym

gymnasium

gymnastics

groundhog

guitar

gymnastics

H h

had

hadn't

hair, hairy

half, halves

hall

hamburger

hammer

hamster

hand

handle

handsome

hang, hanging, hung

happen

happily ever after

happiness

happy

hard

hardware

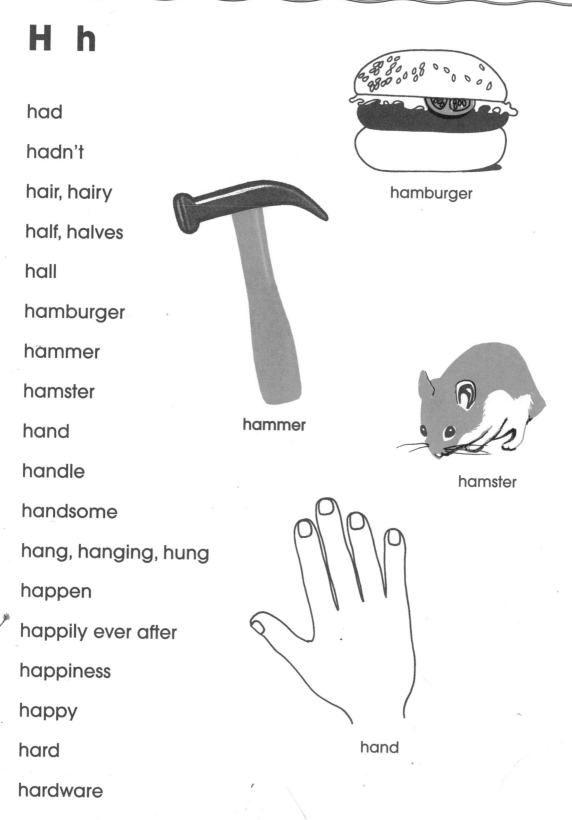

hamburger

hammer

hamster

hand

harm

has

hasn't

hat

hatch

hate

haunt, haunted

have, having, had

haven't

hay

he

head

heap

hear, hearing, heard

heart

heavy

held

helicopter

hello

helmet

hats

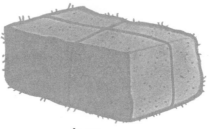

hay

helicopter

helmets

help

hen

her

here

herself

hi

hibernate

hide, hiding, hid, hidden

high

hike, hiking, hiked

hill

him

himself

hippopotamus

his

hit, hitting, hit

hockey   (Look at page 108.)

hold, holding, held

hole

holiday

hen

hiking

hippopotamus

home   (Look at page 109.)

homework

honest

honey

hook

hop, hopping, hopped

hope, hoping, hoped

horn

horse

hospital

hot

hot dog

hotel

hour

house

how

howl

hug, hugging, hugged

huge

human

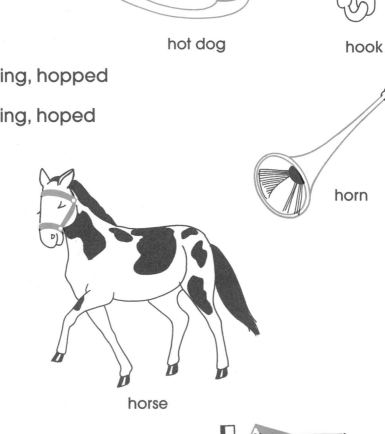

hot dog

hook

horn

horse

house

hungry

hunt

hurray

hurry, hurrying, hurried

hurt, hurting, hurt

husband

ice

I i

ice, icy

ice cream

icing

I'd

idea

if

I'll

ice cream

I'm

imaginary

imagination

important

in

in-line skates

incubator

Indian

injure, injuring, injured

insect   (Look at pages 110 and 111.)

inside

instead

interesting

into

Inuit

invention

invisible

invitation

invite, inviting, invited

is

in-line skates

insects

invitation

island

isn't

it

its

it's

itself

I've

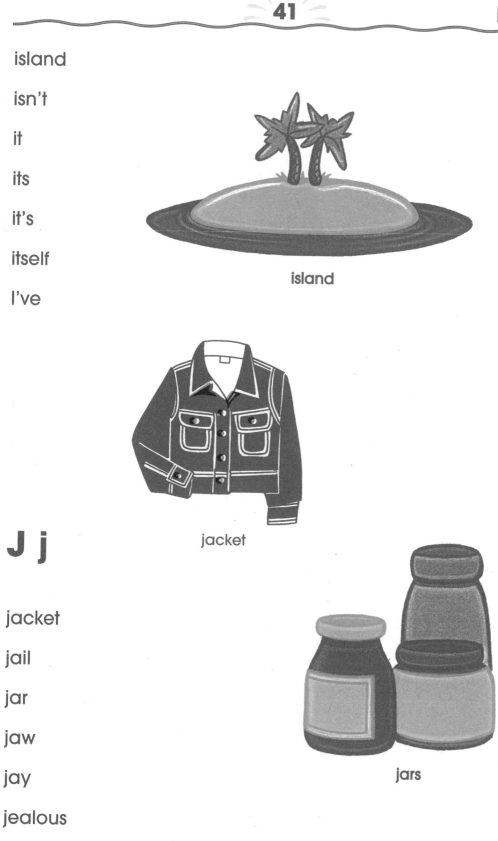

island

jacket

J j

jacket

jail

jar

jaw

jay

jealous

jars

jeans

jelly

jet

jewel, jewellery

join

joke, joking, joked

juice

jump

jungle

junk

just

jeans

jewels

jet

jungle

K k

kangaroo

keep, keeping, kept

keeper

ketchup

key

kick

kid

kill

kind

kindergarten

king

kiss, kisses

kitchen

kite

kitten

knee

kneel, kneeling, knelt

knew

kangaroo

ketchup

keys

kitchen

kites

knife, knives

knight

knock

knot

know, knowing, knew, known

knives

L l

ladder

lady, ladies

ladybug

ladybug

laid

lake

lamb

lamp

land

lamps

large

ladder

laser

last

late, later, latest

laugh

laundry

lawn

lay, laying, laid

lazy

lead, leading, led

leader

leaf, leaves

learn

leather

leave, leaving, left

left

leg

lemon

lemonade

lend, lending, lent

less

laundry

leaves

lemonade

lemons

lesson

let

letter

letter carrier

librarian

library, libraries

lick

lid

lie, lying, lied

lie, lying, lay, lain

lift

light, lighting, lit

lightning

like, liking, liked

line

lion

lip

list

listen

lit

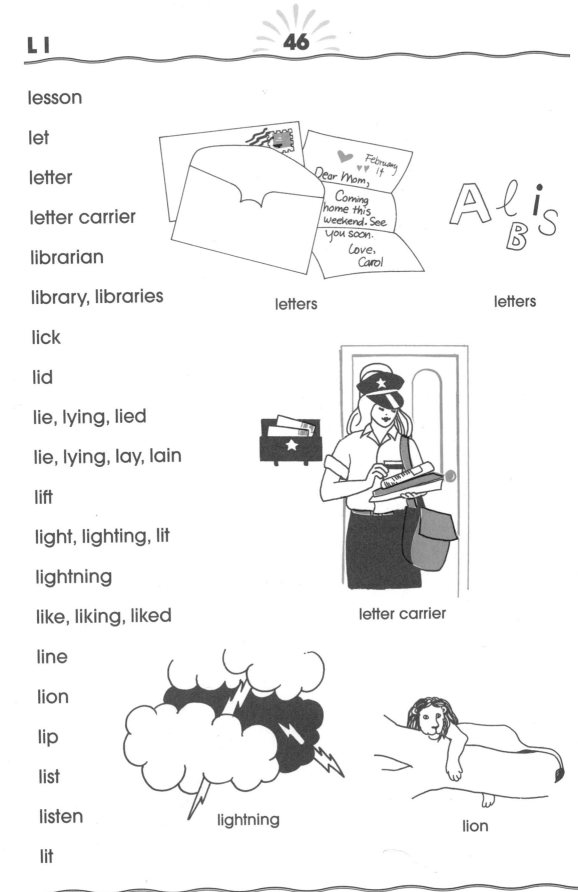

letters

letters

letter carrier

lightning

lion

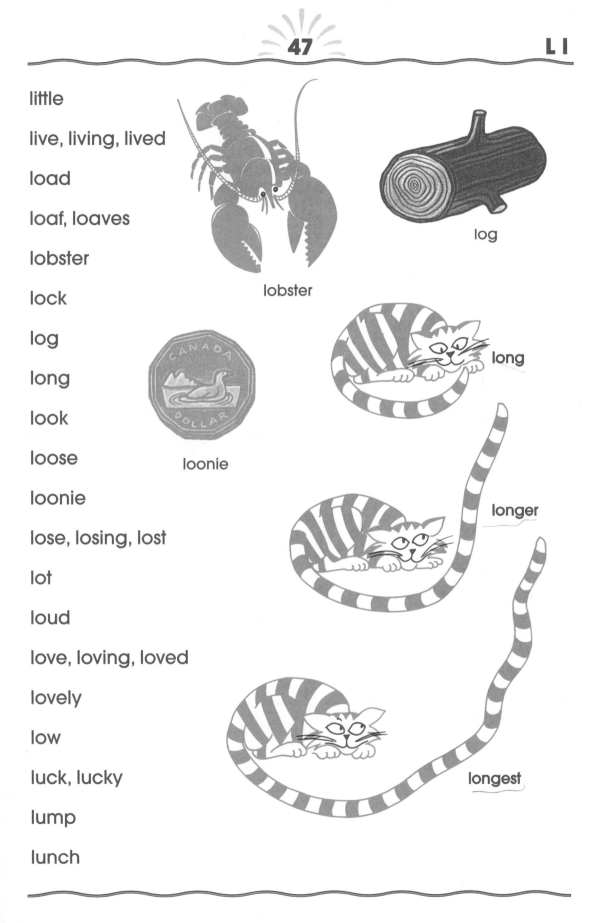

little

live, living, lived

load

loaf, loaves

lobster

lock

log

long

look

loose

loonie

lose, losing, lost

lot

loud

love, loving, loved

lovely

low

luck, lucky

lump

lunch

log

lobster

loonie

long

longer

longest

M m

machine

mad

made

magic

magician

magnet

mail

make, making, made

mall

man, men

many

map

maple

maple syrup

marble

march

mark, marker

market

magnet

map

maple leaves

markers

marry, marrying, married

mask

mass

match, matches

mathematics　(Look at pages 112 and 113.)

matter

may

maybe

me

mean

measles

measure, measuring, measured

meat

medicine

meet, meeting, met

melt

member

men

meow

merry

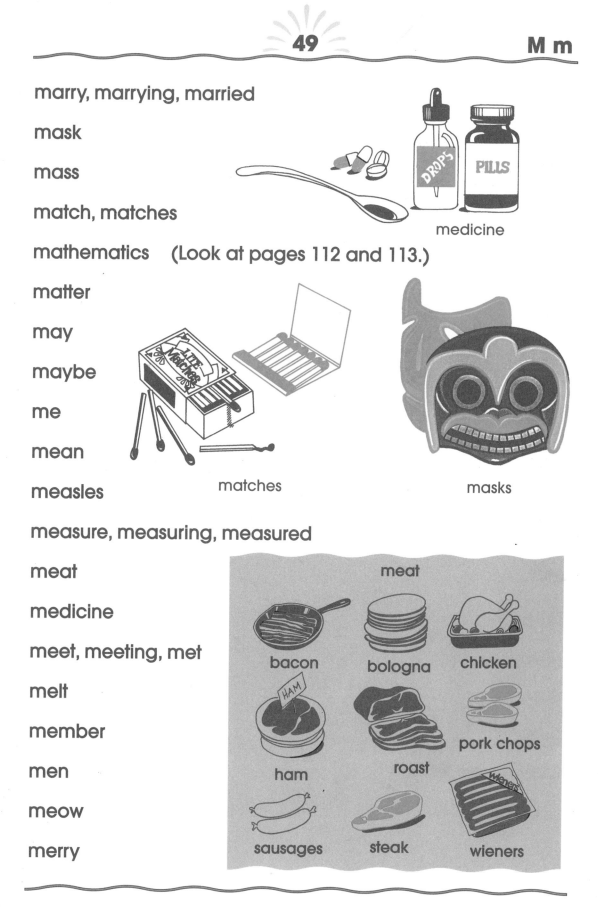

medicine

matches

masks

meat

bacon

bologna

chicken

ham

roast

pork chops

sausages

steak

wieners

mess, messy

met

mice

middle

midnight

might

milk

milk shake

million

mind

mine

minute

mirror

mischief

miss

Miss

mission

mistake

mitt, mitten

mix

mice

milk

milk shake

mirror

mitt

mom

mommy, mommies

money

monkey

monster

month

moo

moon

more

morning

most, mostly

motel

mother

motor

motorcycle

mountain

mouse, mice

mouth

move, moving, moved

movie

money

moon

monkey

mountain

Mr.

Mrs.

Ms.

mud, muddy

mug

mumps

murder

museum

music   (Look at page114.)

must

my

myself

mysterious

mystery, mysteries

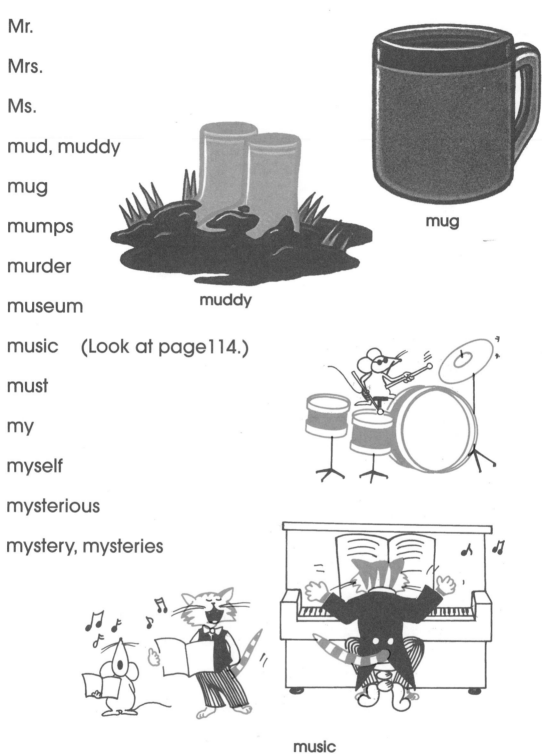

mug

muddy

music

N n

nail

name, naming, named

nap

Native

naughty

near

nearly

neat

neck

need

needle

neighbour, neighbor

neighbourhood, neighborhood

nest

net

never

new

newspaper

nail

nail

needle

newspaper

nest

next

nice

nickel

nickname

night

nightmare

no

nobody

noise, noisy

noodle

noon

no one

north

nose

not

note

nothing

now

number

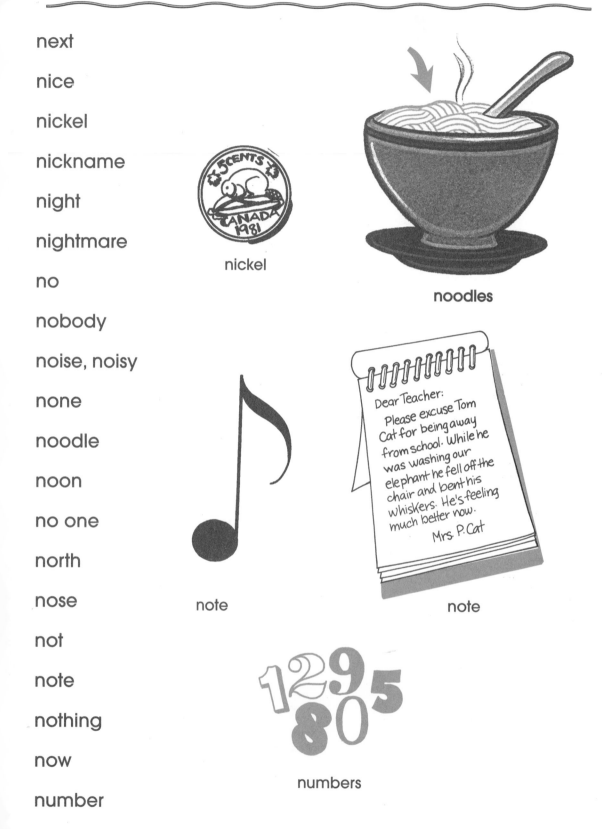

nickel

noodles

note

note

numbers

nurse

nut

nurses

O o

ocean

o'clock

octopus

of

off

office

often

oh

okay

old, older, oldest

on

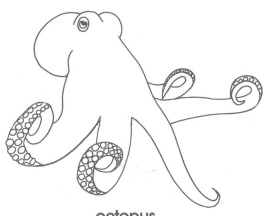

octopus

on   off

once

once upon a time

only

open, opening

or

orange

other

ouch

our

ourselves

out

outside

oven

over

owl

own, owner

oranges

orange juice

orange tree

owl

P p

pack

package

pad

page

paid

pail

pain

paint

pair

palace

pan

pancake

pants

paper

parade

parent

park

parrot

pail

paint

pancakes

parrot

pants

part

party, parties

pass, passing, passed

passenger

past

path

paw

pay, paying, paid

peanut

peanut butter

peek

peep

pencil

penny, pennies

people

perfect

person

pest

pet   (Look at page 115.)

phone

peanuts

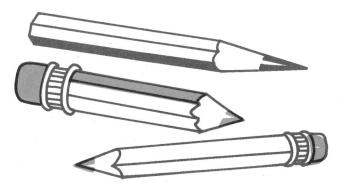

pencils

penny

phone

piano

pick

picnic

picture

pie

piece

pig

pigeon

pile

pillow

pilot

pioneer　(Look at page 116.)

pipe

pirate

pitcher

pizza

place

plan

plane

planet　(Look at page 118.)

piano

pigs

picnic

pigeon

pizza

plane

plant

plate

play, player

playground

plaza

please

pocket

poem

point

poison

pole

police

police officer

pond

pony, ponies

pool

pop

popcorn

porcupine

porridge

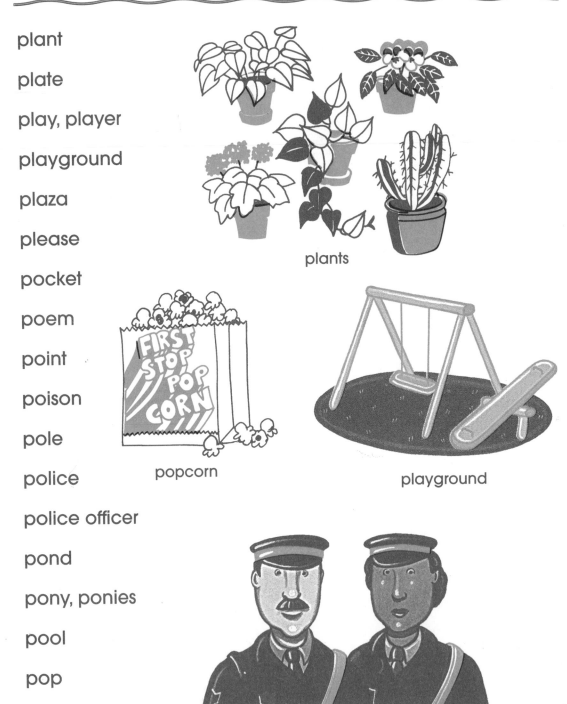

plants

popcorn

playground

police officers

possible

post office

pot

potato, potatoes

pour

power

practice, practise

pray, prayer

present

pretend

pretty, prettier, prettiest

price

prince

princess

principal

print, printer

prize

problem

program

project

pot

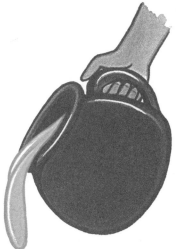

pour

potatoes

promise

protect

proud

puck

pudding

puddle

pull

pumpkin

pupil

puppet

puppy, puppies

purr

purse

push

pussy

put, putting, put

puzzle

pyjamas, pajamas

puddle

puppets

pumpkin

puzzle

pyjamas

Q q

quack

quarter

queen

question

quick, quickly

quiet, quietly

quit, quitting, quit

quarter

quarter

queen

question mark

R r

rabbit

raccoon

race, racing, raced

radio

railroad

rain, rainy

rainbow

raincoat

raise, raising, raised

ran

ranch, ranches

rang

rat

rather

ray

reach

read, reading, read

reader

rabbit

raccoon

radio and tape player

raincoat

ready

real

really

reason

recess

recipe

record, recorder

remember

remote

rent

repair

rescue, rescuing, rescued

rest

restaurant

return

reward

rhyme

ribbon

rice

rich

restaurant

rice

ribbon

rid

riddle

ride, riding, rode, ridden

right

ring

rip, ripping, ripped

river

road

roar

roast

rob, robbing, robbed

robber

robin

robot

rock

rocket

rod

rode

rodeo

roll

ring

river

rocket

robin

roller coaster

roller skates

roof, roofs (rooves)

room

rooster

root

rope

rough

round

row

rowboat

rub, rubbing, rubbed

rubber

rug

ruin

ruler

run, running, ran, run

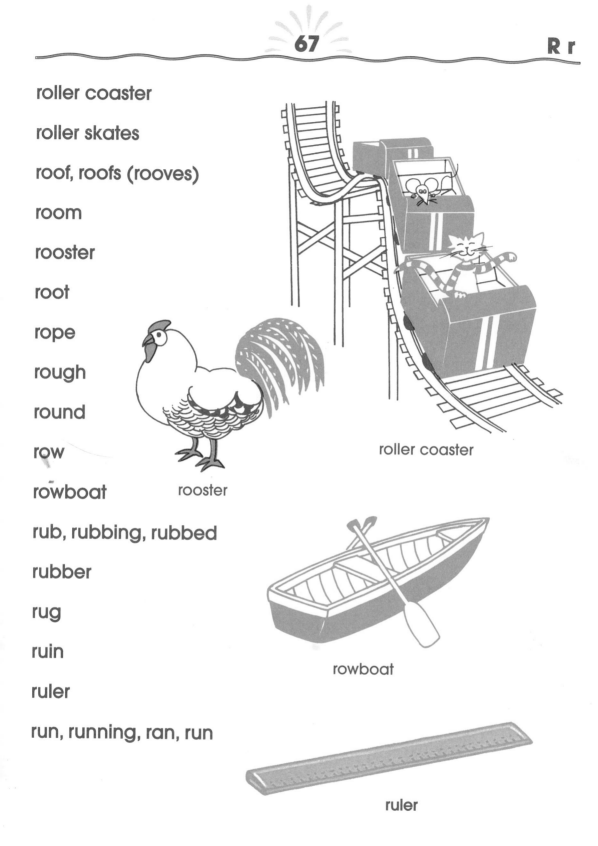

roller coaster

rooster

rowboat

ruler

S s

sack

sad

saddle

safe, safety

said

sail

sailboat

sailor

salad

sale

same

sand

sandwich, sandwiches

sang

Santa Claus

sat

save, saving, saved

saw

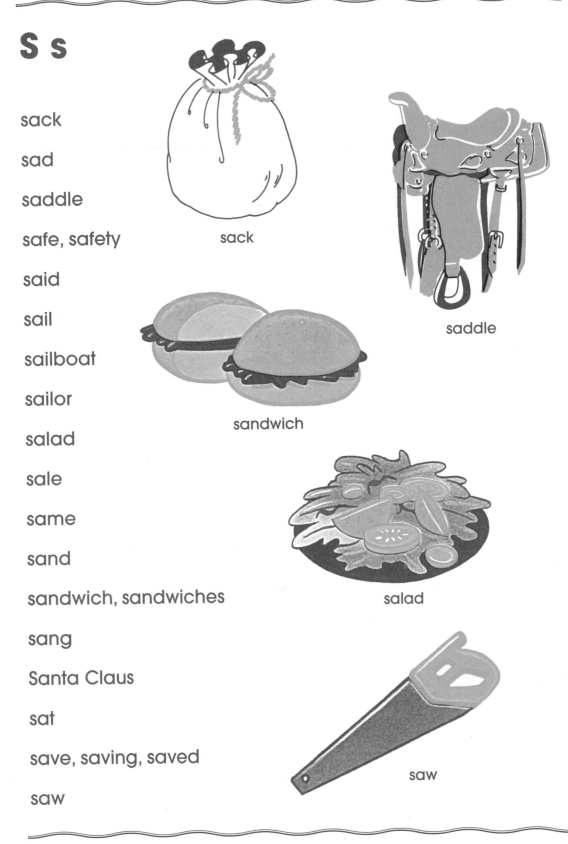

sack

saddle

sandwich

salad

saw

say, saying, said

scare, scaring, scared

scarecrow

scary

school

schoolyard

science

scissors

score, scoring, scored

scrap

scrape

scratch

scream

scrub, scrubbing, scrubbed

sea   (Look at page 117.)

seal

seat

second

secret

see, seeing, saw, seen

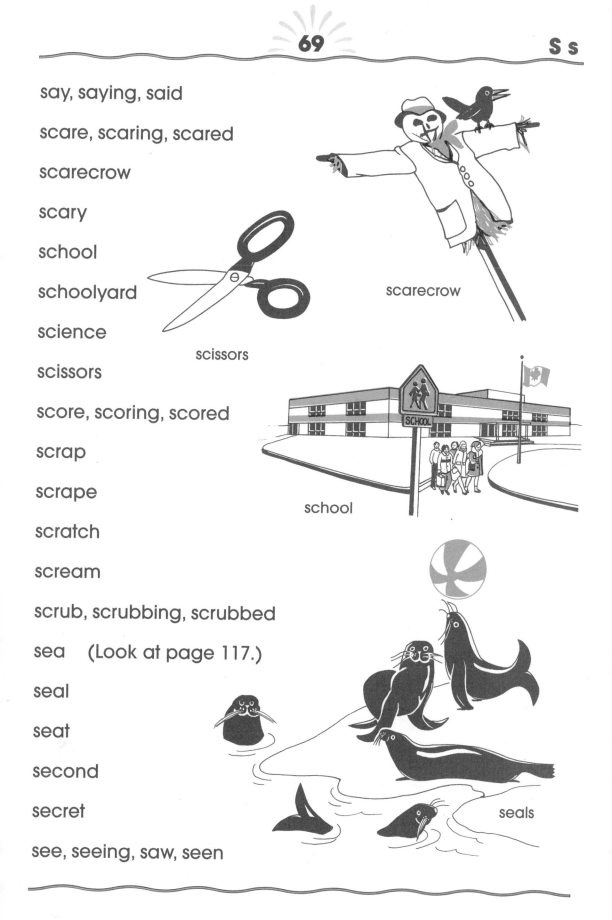

scarecrow

scissors

school

seals

seed

seen

sell, selling, sold

send, sending, sent

separate, separated

set

sew

shadow

shake, shaking, shook, shaken

shall

shape

share, sharing, shared

shark

sharp

she

sheep

sheet

shelf, shelves

shell

shine, shining, shone

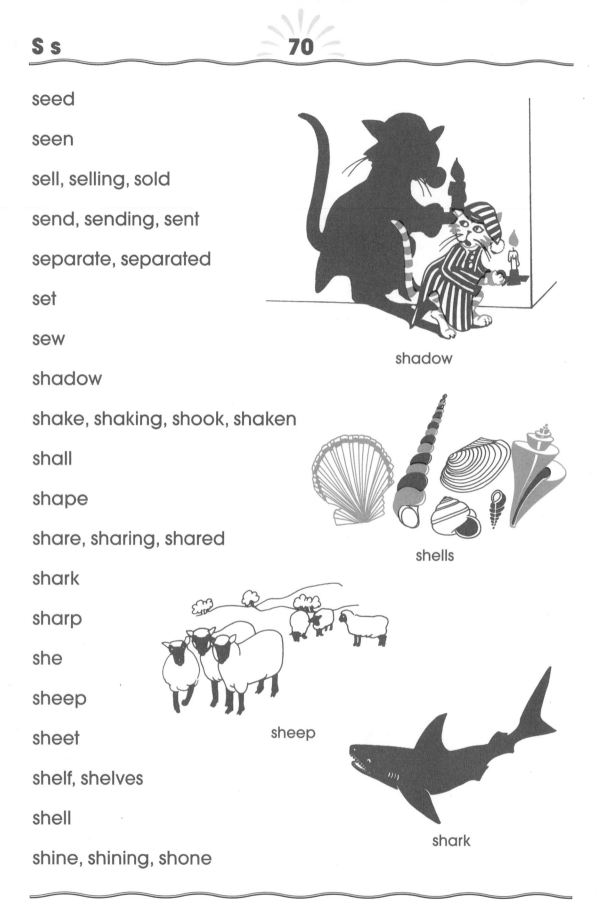

shadow

shells

sheep

shark

shiny

ship

shirt

shoe

shook

shoot, shooting, shot

shop, shopping, shopped

shopping centre

short

shot

should

shouldn't

shout

show, showing, shown

shower

shut, shutting, shut

sick

side

sidewalk

sign

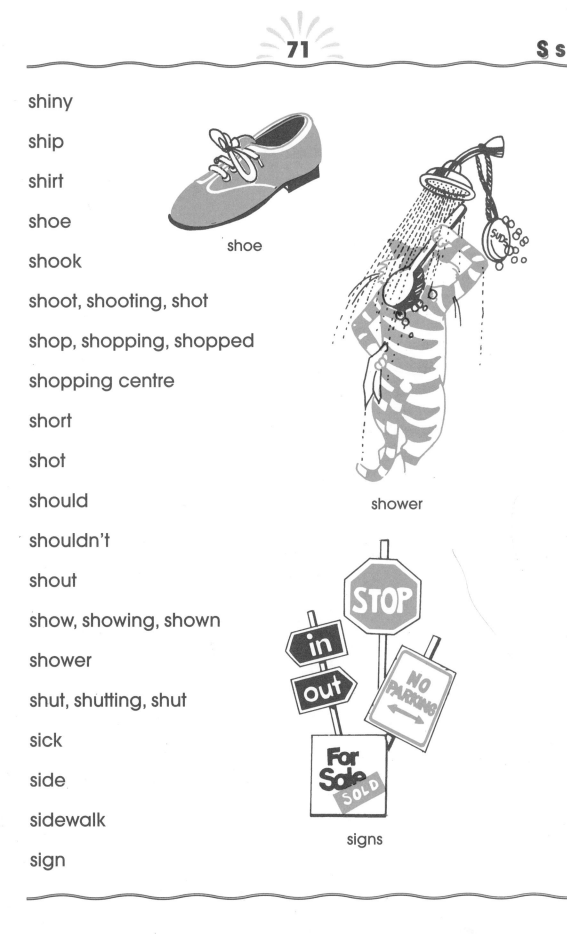

shoe

shower

signs

silly

silver

simple

sing, singing, sang, sung

sink, sinking, sank, sunk

sister

sit, sitting, sat

size

skate, skating, skated

skateboard

skeleton

ski, skiing, skied

skin, skinny

skip, skipping, skipped

skirt

skunk

sky, skies

slam, slamming, slammed

sled

sleep, sleeping, slept

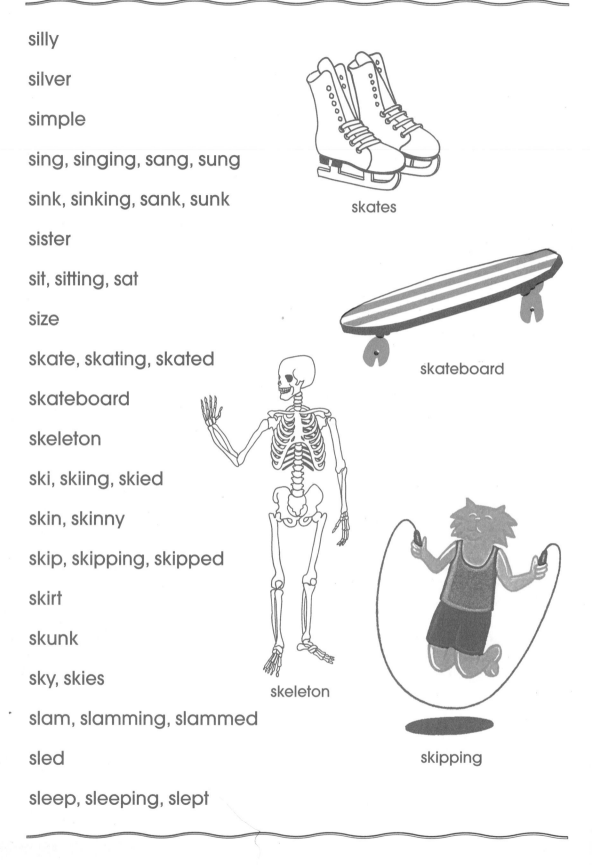

skates

skateboard

skeleton

skipping

sleepy

sleigh

slide, sliding, slid

slip, slipping, slipped

slipper

slow

small

smart

smash

smell

smile, smiling, smiled

smoke

smooth

snake

sneak, sneaking, sneaked (snuck)

sneaker

sneaky

sneeze, sneezing, sneezed

sniff

snore, snoring, snored

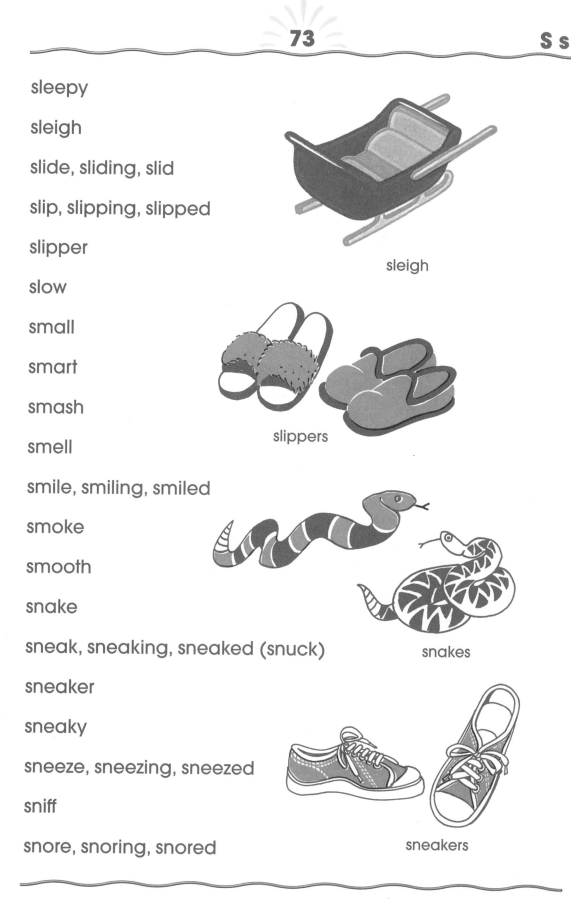

sleigh

slippers

snakes

sneakers

snow, snowy

snowball

snowflake

snowman

so

soap

soccer

sock

soft

software

sold

soldier

some

somebody

someone

something

sometimes

somewhere

son

song

snowflakes

snowman

soap

soccer

socks

soon

sore

sorry

sort

sound

soup

south

space   (Look at page 118.)

spank

speak, speaking, spoke, spoken

special

speed

spell

spend, spending, spent

spider

spill

splash

spoke

spooky

spoon

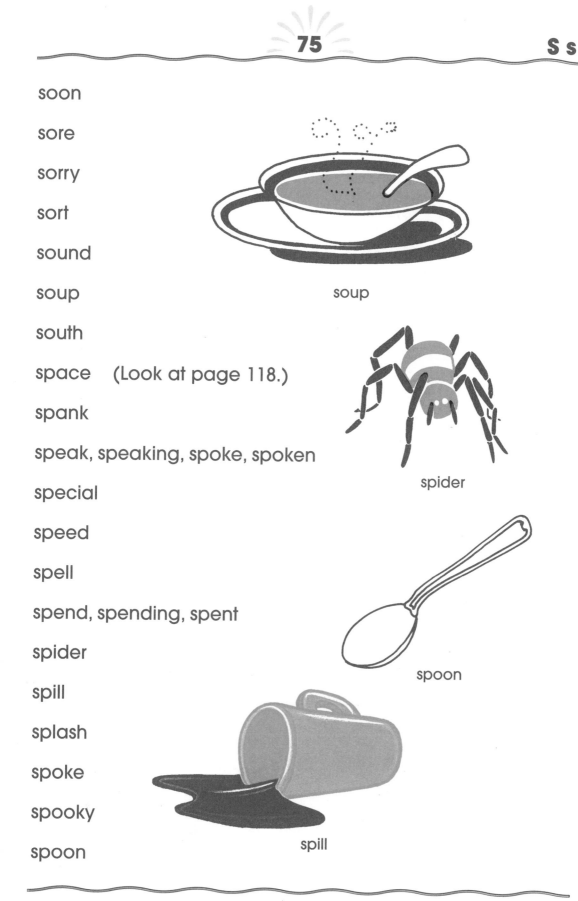

soup

spider

spoon

spill

sport   (Look at page 119.)

spot

spring

spy, spying, spied

square

square

squeak

squirrel

squirrel

squirt

stage

stair

stake

stamp

stand, standing, stood

stamps

star

start

starve, starving, starved

station

stay

steak

steal, stealing, stole, stolen

steak

step

stick

still

sting

stir, stirring, stirred

stole, stolen

stomach, stomachache

stone

stood

stop, stopping, stopped

store

storm

story, stories

stove

straight

strange, stranger

straw

stream

street

stretch

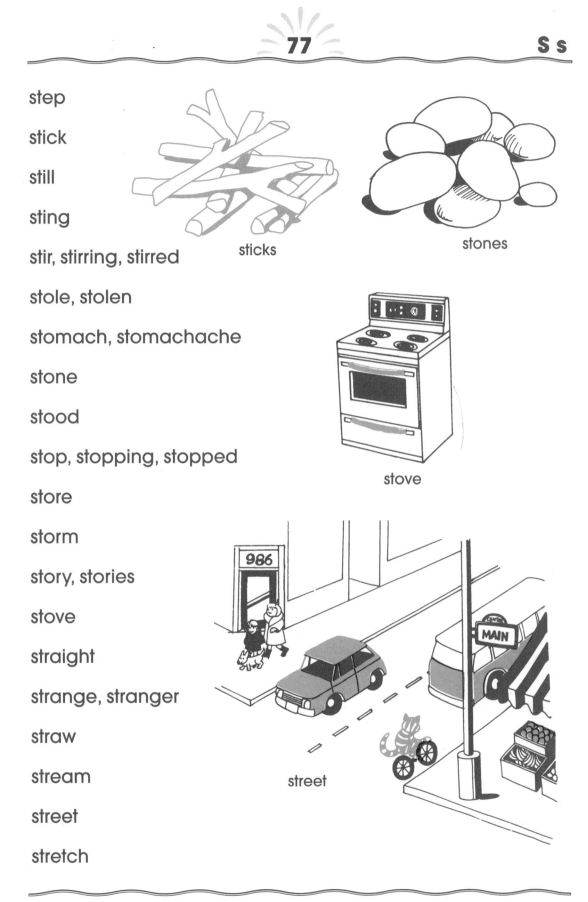

sticks

stones

stove

street

string

stripe

strong

stuck

stuff

stupid

submarine

such

suck

sudden, suddenly

sugar

suit

summer

sun, sunny

sunburn

sundae

sunshine

super

supermarket

supper

submarine

suit

sundae

sun

supermarket

suppose, supposing, supposed

sure

surprise

sweat

sweater

sweet

swim, swimming, swam, swum

swimmer

swing

sword

syrup

system

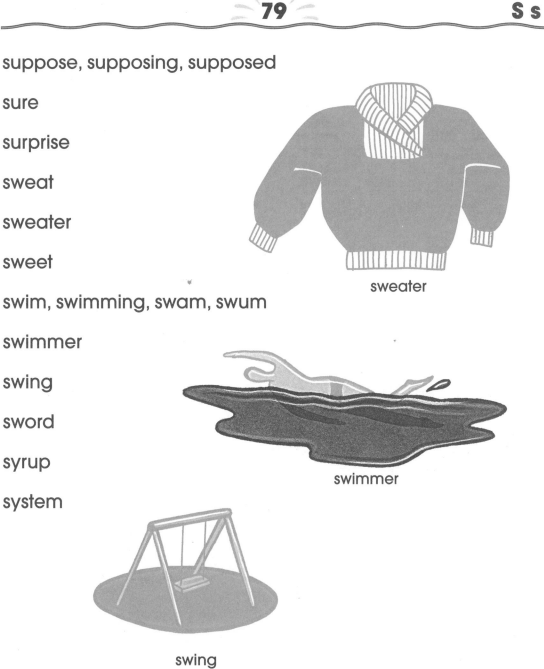

sweater

swimmer

swing

T t

table

tadpole

tag

tail

take, taking, took, taken

tale

talk

tall

tame

tank

tap

tape

tape-recorder

taste, tasting, tasted

taught

taxi

teach, teaching, taught

teacher

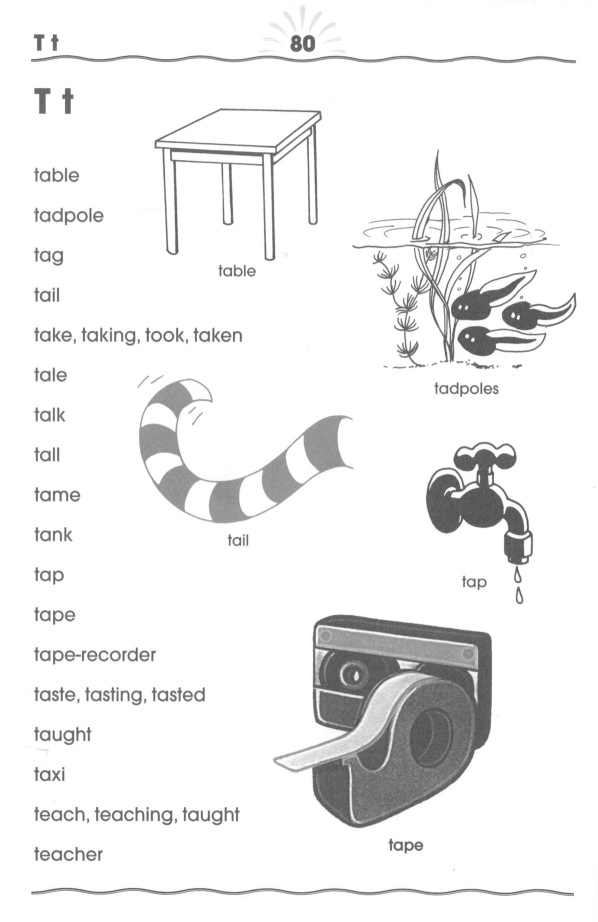

table

tadpoles

tail

tap

tape

team

tear

tear, tearing, tore, torn

tease, teasing, teased

teeth

telephone

telescope

television

telescope

tell, telling, told

television

tent

terrarium

terrible

terrific

test

than

tent

thank

thankful

thank you

that

the

terrarium

their

them

themselves

then

there

these

they

thick

thief, thieves

thin, thinner, thinnest

thing

think, thinking, thought

thirsty

this

those

thought

threw

throne

through

throw, throwing, threw, thrown

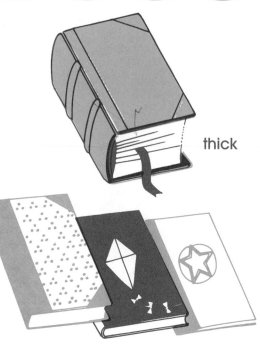

thick

thin, thinner, thinnest

thirsty

throne

thumb

thunder

ticket

tickle, tickling, tickled

tie, tying, tied

tiger

till

time

tiny, tinier, tiniest

tire, tired

title

to

toad

toast

toboggan

today

toe

together

told

tomorrow

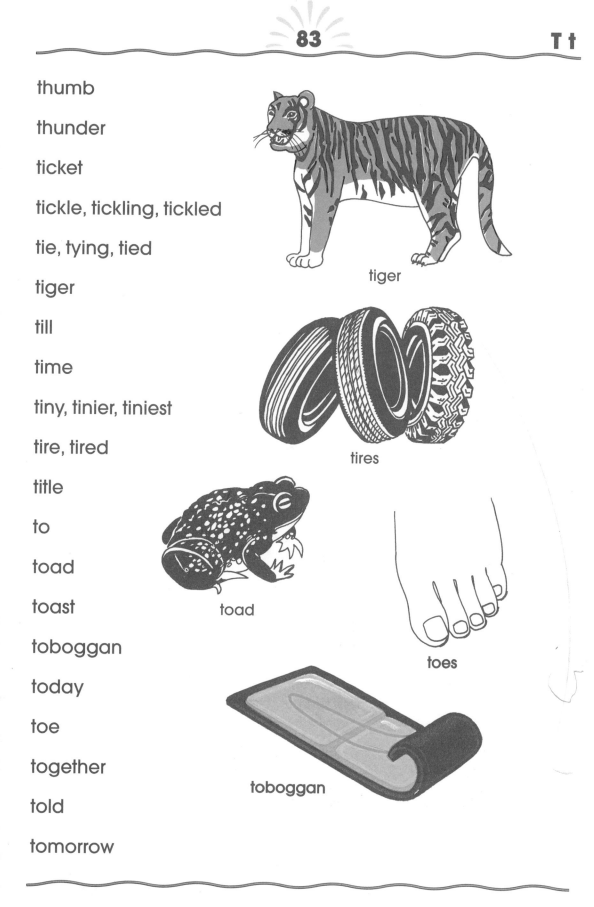

tiger

tires

toad

toes

toboggan

tongue

tonight

too

took

tool

tooth, teeth

toothbrush

toothpaste

toothbrush

top

torn

touch

tow

towards

toothpaste

towel

town

toy

track

town

trade, trading, traded

trail, trailer

train

trailer

trampoline

transportation   (Look at pages 120 and 121.)

trap, trapping, trapped

travel, travelling, travelled

treasure

treat

tree

triangle

trick

tried

trip, tripping, tripped

troll

trouble

truck

true

trunk

trust

truth

try, trying, tried

T-shirt

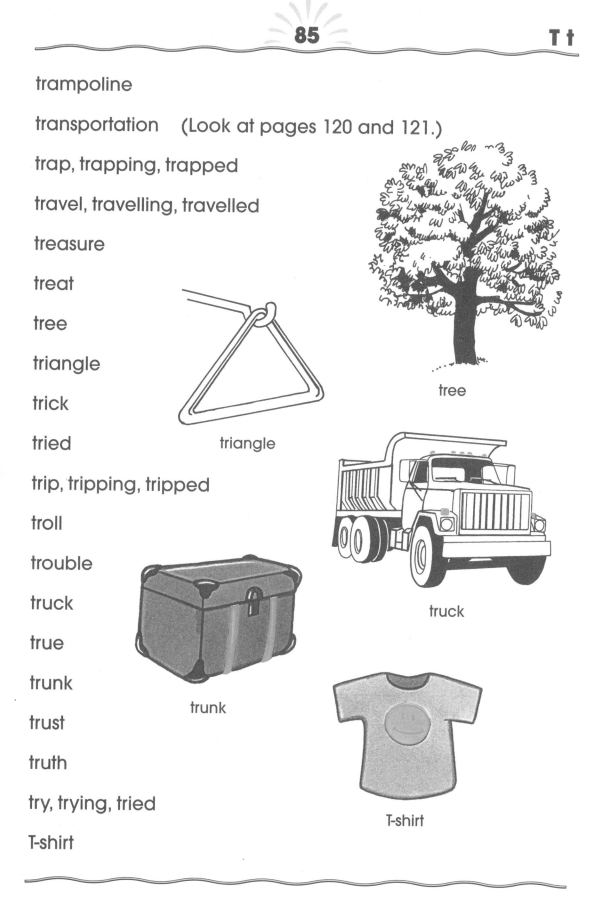

triangle

tree

truck

trunk

T-shirt

tube

tune

tunnel

turkey

turn

turtle

twice

tunnel

turkey

turtle

U u

ugly, uglier, ugliest

umbrella

uncle

under

understand, understanding, understood

underwear

unhappy

unless

until

up

upon

upset

upside down

upstairs

us

use, using, used

usually

umbrella

underwear

upside down

upstairs

V v

vacation

valentine

vampire

van

vanish

VCR

vegetable

veterinarian

video

village

violent

visit, visitor

voice

volcano, volcanoes

voyage

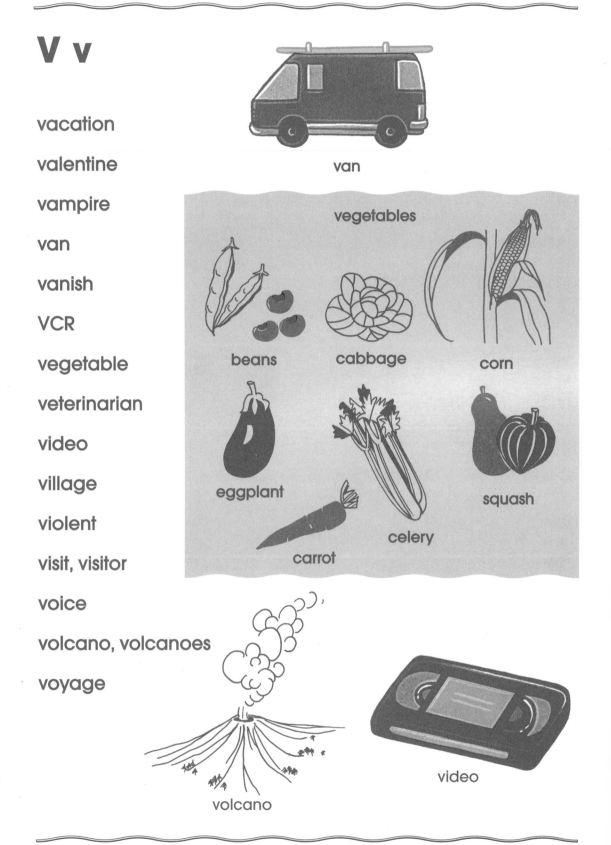

van

vegetables

beans

cabbage

corn

eggplant

carrot

celery

squash

volcano

video

W w

wade, wading, waded

wag, wagging, wagged

wagon

wait, waiter, waitress

wake, waking, woke, woken

walk

wall

wallet

walrus

wand

war

warm

was

wash

washroom

wasn't

waste

watch, watches

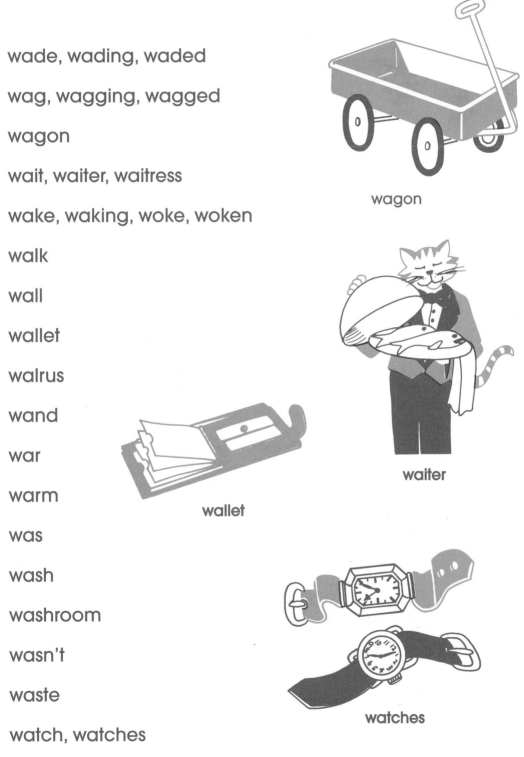

wagon

waiter

wallet

watches

water

wave, waving, waved

way

we

weak

weak

wear, wearing, wore, worn

weather   (Look at pages 122 and 123.)

wedding

week

week

weekend

weigh

weight

weird

welcome

well

went

well

wet

were

weren't

west

wet

whale

what

wheel

when

whenever

where

which

while

whip, whipping, whipped

whiskers

whisper

whistle, whistling, whistled

who, whom

whole

who's

whose

why

wicked

wide

width

wheel

whiskers

whistle

wife, wives

wiggle, wiggling, wiggled

wild

will

win, winning, won

wind

wind, winding, wound

window

wing

wink

winner

winter

wipe

wise

wish, wishes

with

without

wizard

woke

wolf, wolves

wing

window

wolf

wink

woman, women

won

wonder

wonderful

won't

wood

wool

word

wore

work

worker

world

worm

worry, worrying, worried

worse

worst

would

wouldn't

wound

wrap, wrapping, wrapped

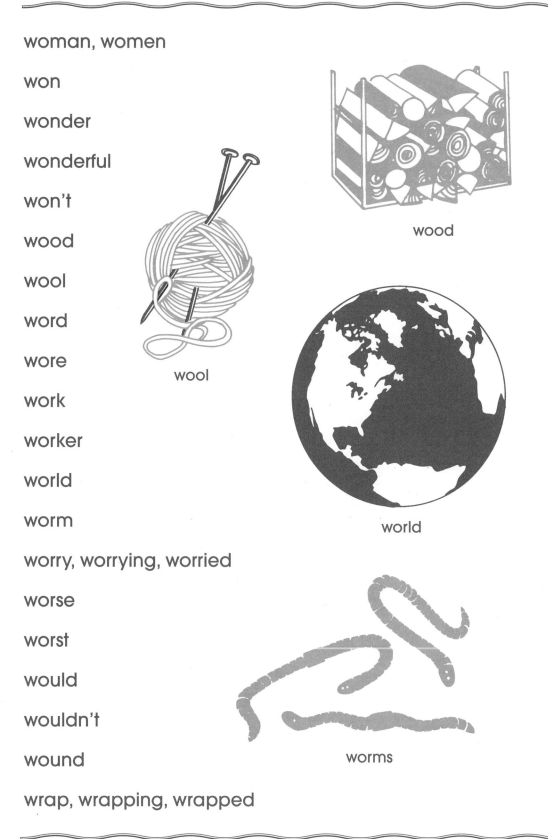

wood

wool

world

worms

wrap, wrapping, wrapped

wreck

wrinkle

wrist

write, writing, wrote, written

wrong

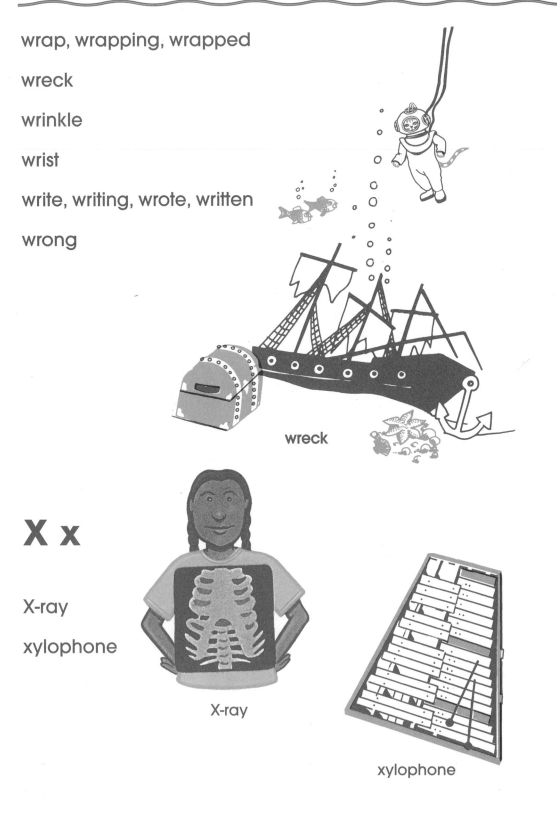

wreck

X x

X-ray

xylophone

X-ray

xylophone

Y y

yard

yarn

yawn

year

yell

yes

yesterday

yet

you

you'd

you'll

young

your

you're

yourself

you've

yo-yo

yarn

yawn

young　　younger　　youngest

yo-yo

Z z

zebra

zero

zipper

zoo

zoom

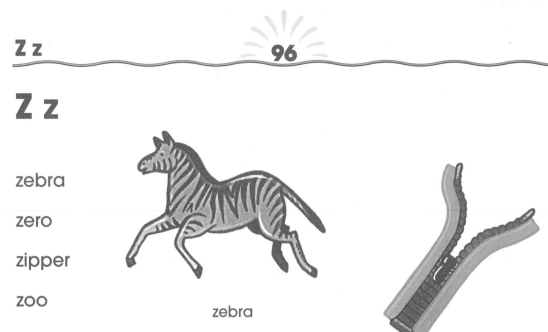

zebra

zipper

zoo

97

Baseball

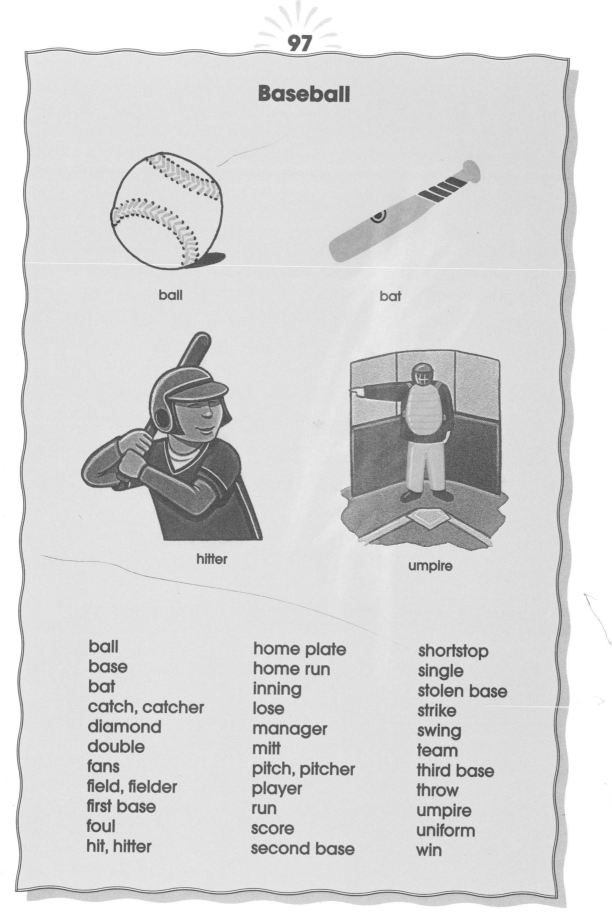

ball

bat

hitter

umpire

ball
base
bat
catch, catcher
diamond
double
fans
field, fielder
first base
foul
hit, hitter

home plate
home run
inning
lose
manager
mitt
pitch, pitcher
player
run
score
second base

shortstop
single
stolen base
strike
swing
team
third base
throw
umpire
uniform
win

The Body

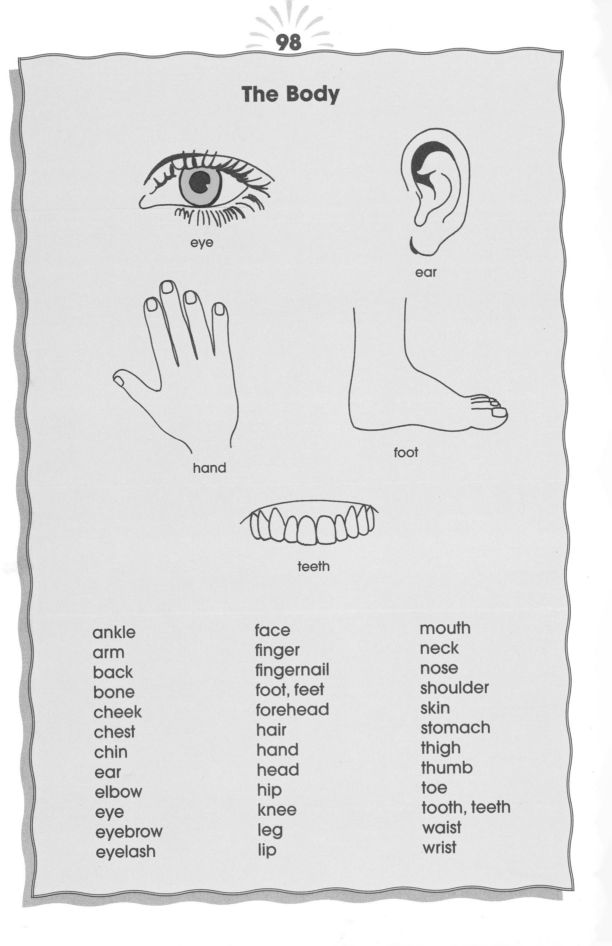

eye

ear

hand

foot

teeth

ankle	face	mouth
arm	finger	neck
back	fingernail	nose
bone	foot, feet	shoulder
cheek	forehead	skin
chest	hair	stomach
chin	hand	thigh
ear	head	thumb
elbow	hip	toe
eye	knee	tooth, teeth
eyebrow	leg	waist
eyelash	lip	wrist

Castle Days

knight

princess   prince

sword

castle

armour, armor	joust	peasant
castle	king	prince
chainmail	knight	princess
church	lady, ladies	queen
coat of arms	lance	shield
cottage	long ago	suit of armour
drawbridge	lord	sword
dungeon	manor	tournament
falcon	medieval	tower
feast	Middle Ages	turret
great hall	mill	village
horse	moat	
jester	page	

Celebrations

Advent
April Fool's Day
Baisakhi
birthday
Canada Day
Ch'ing Ming
    Festival
Ch'usok
    Chusongnal
Dia de la Raza
Divali
Easter
Epiphany
Father's Day
Festival of Lights
Good Friday
Green Corn
    Festival
Groundhog Day
Hallowe'en

Hanukkah

Hana Matsuri	Rosh Hashana
Hanukkah	Shichi-go-san
Jamshedi Navroz	Shiva Ratri
May Day	Solnal
Moon Festival	Songkran
Mother's Day	St-Jean Baptiste
Mummering	Day
Navaratri	St. Lucia Day
New Year's Day	St. Nicholas Day
Now Ruz	St. Patrick's Day
Oktoberfest	Sukkot
Ohigan	Tet Festival
Passover	Thanksgiving
Pongal	Toonik Tyme
Powwow	Twelfth Night
Purim	Valentine's Day
Ramadan	Victoria Day
Ram Navami	Wesak
Remembrance	Yom Kippur
Day	

Some Celebration Words

Christmas
Boxing Day
carols
Jesus
lights
presents
reindeer
Santa Claus
tree
turkey dinner

tree

Santa Claus

Kwanza
candles
feast
gifts
seven
unity cup
visits

candles

Holi
bonfires
dancing
harvest
Krishna
necklaces
singing
tika

bonfire

Xin nian (Chinese New Year)
Dragon Dance
Festival of Lights
firecrackers
li shee
Lion Dance
money tree

Dragon Dance

The Community

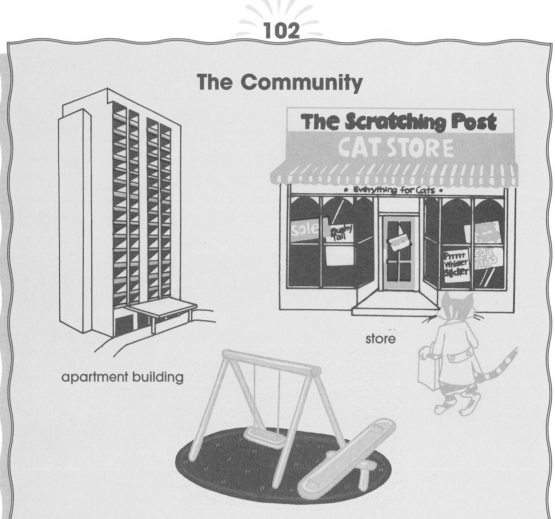

apartment building

store

playground

ambulance	house	police officer
apartment	letter carrier	post office
bank	mall	road
buildings	mayor	school
church	mosque	shop
city, cities	neighbour,	sidewalk
citizen	neighbor	store
community centre	neighbourhood,	street
factory, factories	neighborhood	synagogue
fairground	office building	road
firefighter	park	town
garbage collector	playground	village
home	plaza	
hospital	people	

Dinosaurs

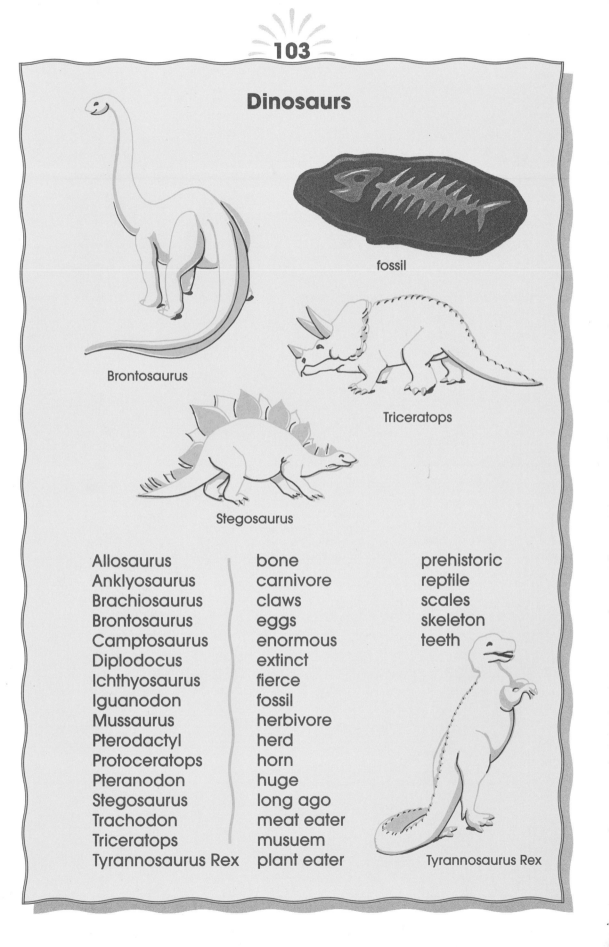

fossil

Brontosaurus

Triceratops

Stegosaurus

Allosaurus	bone	prehistoric
Anklyosaurus	carnivore	reptile
Brachiosaurus	claws	scales
Brontosaurus	eggs	skeleton
Camptosaurus	enormous	teeth
Diplodocus	extinct	
Ichthyosaurus	fierce	
Iguanodon	fossil	
Mussaurus	herbivore	
Pterodactyl	herd	
Protoceratops	horn	
Pteranodon	huge	
Stegosaurus	long ago	
Trachodon	meat eater	
Triceratops	musuem	
Tyrannosaurus Rex	plant eater	

Tyrannosaurus Rex

The Environment

forest

animal	endangered species
acid rain	energy
air	extinct, extinction
bird	forest
compost	habitat
conservation	insect
danger	lake
destroy	marsh
earth	ocean
endanger,	planet
endangered	plants

river

pollution
pond
protect, protection
rain
rainforest
recycle
reduce
reptile
resources
reuse
river

save
solar
swamp
tropical
waste
water
wetlands
wildlife

Families

families

adopted	grandmother	nephew
aunt, auntie	grandpa	niece
baby, babies	grandparents	parent
brother	granny	sister
care	half brother	share
cousin	half sister	son
dad, daddy	help	stepbrother
daughter	love	stepfather
father	member	stepmother
family	mom, mommy	stepsister
grandad	mother	together
grandfather	mum, mummy	uncle
grandma	nana	

The Farm

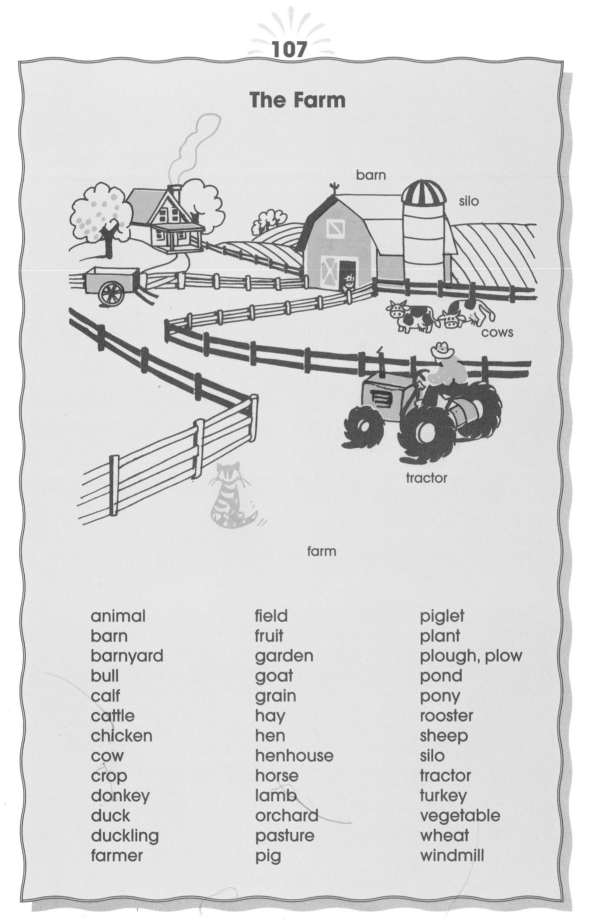

barn

silo

cows

tractor

farm

animal	field	piglet
barn	fruit	plant
barnyard	garden	plough, plow
bull	goat	pond
calf	grain	pony
cattle	hay	rooster
chicken	hen	sheep
cow	henhouse	silo
crop	horse	tractor
donkey	lamb	turkey
duck	orchard	vegetable
duckling	pasture	wheat
farmer	pig	windmill

Hockey

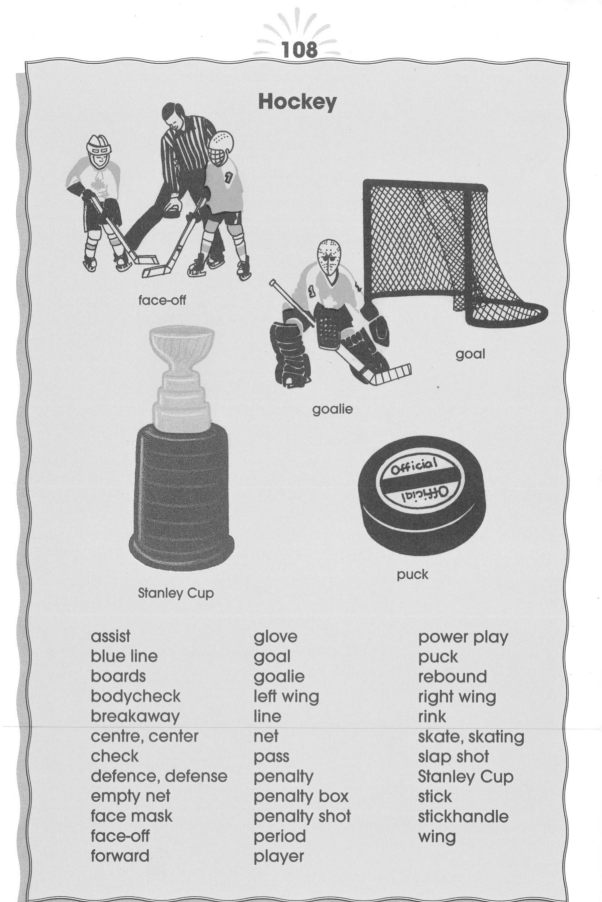

face-off

goalie

goal

Stanley Cup

puck

assist	glove	power play
blue line	goal	puck
boards	goalie	rebound
bodycheck	left wing	right wing
breakaway	line	rink
centre, center	net	skate, skating
check	pass	slap shot
defence, defense	penalty	Stanley Cup
empty net	penalty box	stick
face mask	penalty shot	stickhandle
face-off	period	wing
forward	player	

Homes

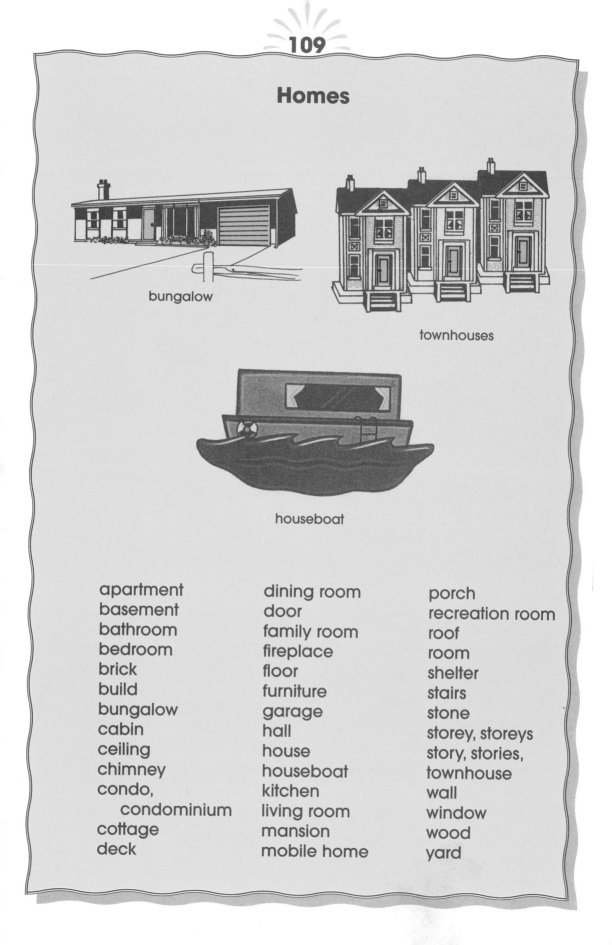

bungalow

townhouses

houseboat

apartment	dining room	porch
basement	door	recreation room
bathroom	family room	roof
bedroom	fireplace	room
brick	floor	shelter
build	furniture	stairs
bungalow	garage	stone
cabin	hall	storey, storeys
ceiling	house	story, stories,
chimney	houseboat	townhouse
condo,	kitchen	wall
condominium	living room	window
cottage	mansion	wood
deck	mobile home	yard

Insects and Other Crawlers

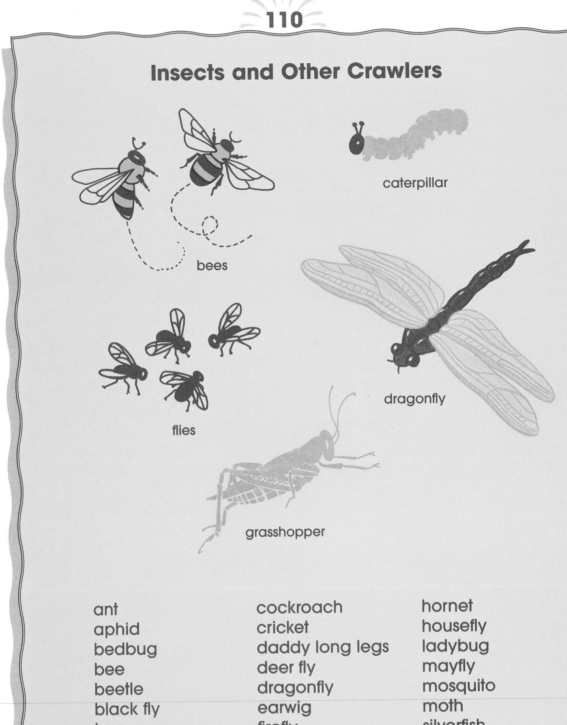

bees

caterpillar

flies

dragonfly

grasshopper

ant	cockroach	hornet
aphid	cricket	housefly
bedbug	daddy long legs	ladybug
bee	deer fly	mayfly
beetle	dragonfly	mosquito
black fly	earwig	moth
bug	firefly	silverfish
bumblebee	flea	sawbug
butterfly	fly, flies	spider
caterpillar	fruit fly	walking stick
centipede	grasshopper	wasp
cicada	honeybee	

Some Insect Words

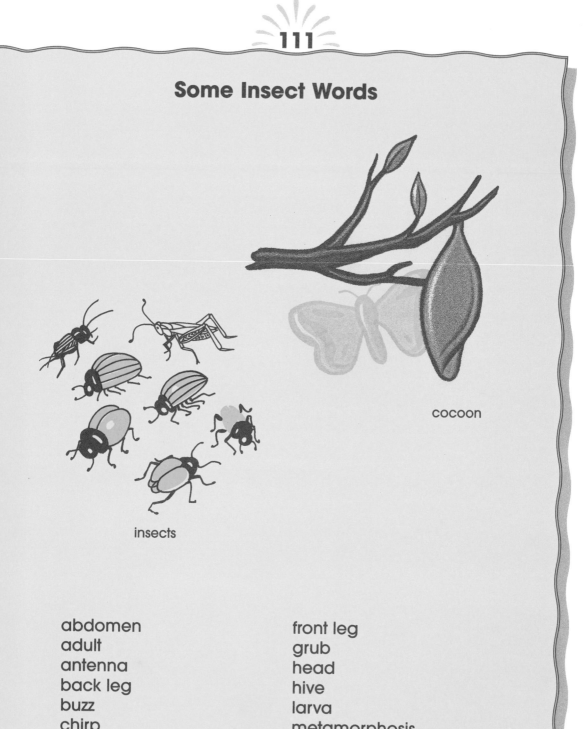

cocoon

insects

abdomen	front leg
adult	grub
antenna	head
back leg	hive
buzz	larva
chirp	metamorphosis
cocoon	middle leg
collect	mouth parts
colony	nest
compound eye	pupa
egg	thorax
eye	wing

Mathematics

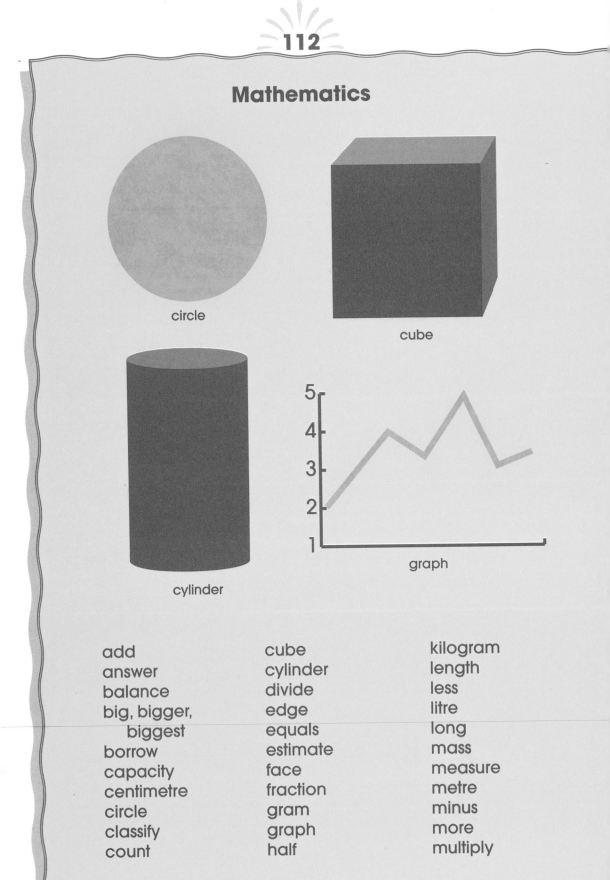

circle

cube

cylinder

graph

add	cube	kilogram
answer	cylinder	length
balance	divide	less
big, bigger,	edge	litre
biggest	equals	long
borrow	estimate	mass
capacity	face	measure
centimetre	fraction	metre
circle	gram	minus
classify	graph	more
count	half	multiply

square

triangle

rectangle

number	set	square
numeral	shape	subtract
order	short	surface
pattern	side	symmetry
place value	size	triangle
plus	small	unit
problem	solid	volume
rectangle	sort	wide
rule	space	width
second	sphere	zero

Music

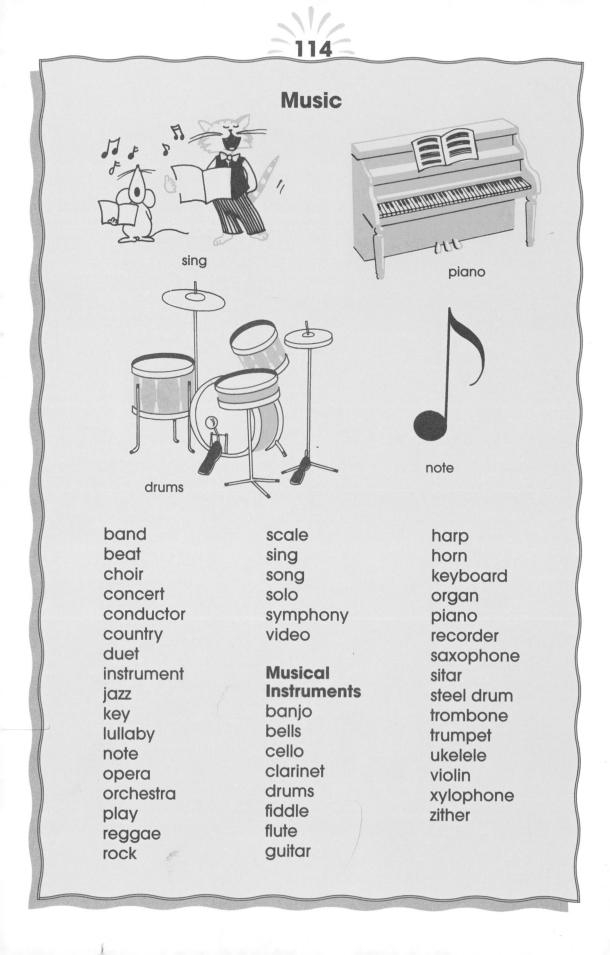

sing

piano

drums

note

band	scale	harp
beat	sing	horn
choir	song	keyboard
concert	solo	organ
conductor	symphony	piano
country	video	recorder
duet		saxophone
instrument	**Musical**	sitar
jazz	**Instruments**	steel drum
key	banjo	trombone
lullaby	bells	trumpet
note	cello	ukelele
opera	clarinet	violin
orchestra	drums	xylophone
play	fiddle	zither
reggae	flute	
rock	guitar	

Pets

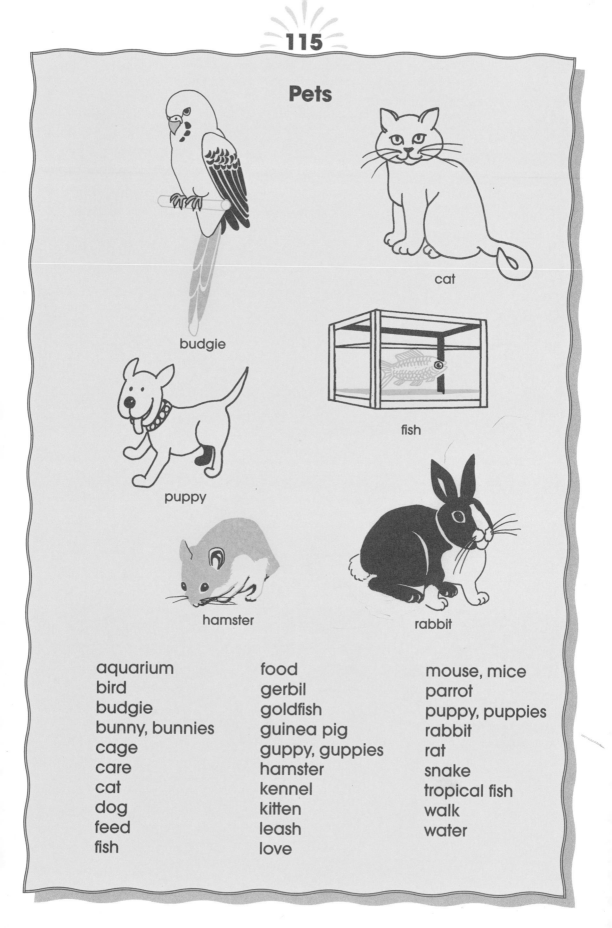

budgie

cat

fish

puppy

hamster

rabbit

aquarium	food	mouse, mice
bird	gerbil	parrot
budgie	goldfish	puppy, puppies
bunny, bunnies	guinea pig	rabbit
cage	guppy, guppies	rat
care	hamster	snake
cat	kennel	tropical fish
dog	kitten	walk
feed	leash	water
fish	love	

Pioneers

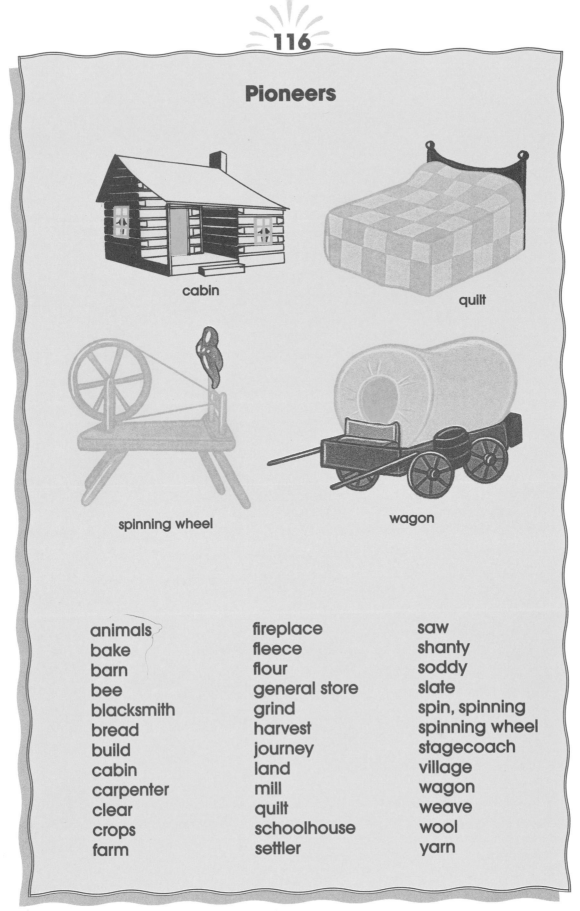

cabin

quilt

spinning wheel

wagon

animals	fireplace	saw
bake	fleece	shanty
barn	flour	soddy
bee	general store	slate
blacksmith	grind	spin, spinning
bread	harvest	spinning wheel
build	journey	stagecoach
cabin	land	village
carpenter	mill	wagon
clear	quilt	weave
crops	schoolhouse	wool
farm	settler	yarn

The Sea

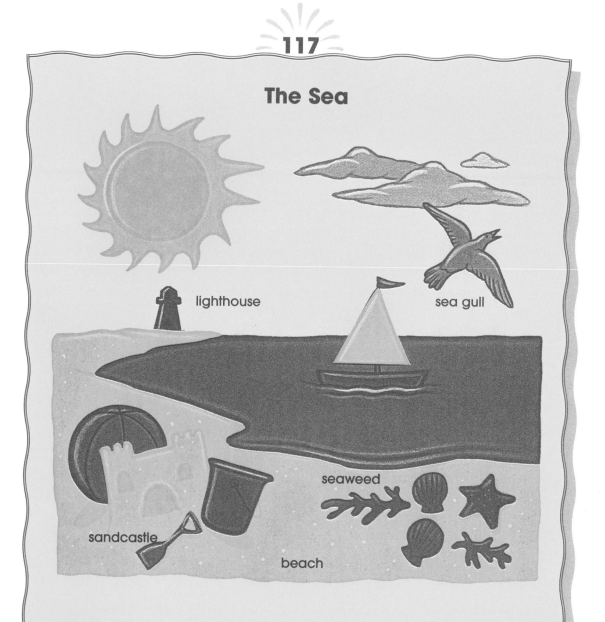

lighthouse

sea gull

seaweed

sandcastle

beach

bay	ocean	seashore
beach	octopus	seaside
boat	pier	seaweed
breakers	port	ship
cliff	rocks	shipwreck
cove	salt	shore
dock	sand	starfish
dunes	sandcastle	surf
fish	seal	tide
harbour, harbor	sea gull	underwater
island	sea horse	water
lighthouse	seashells	wave

Space

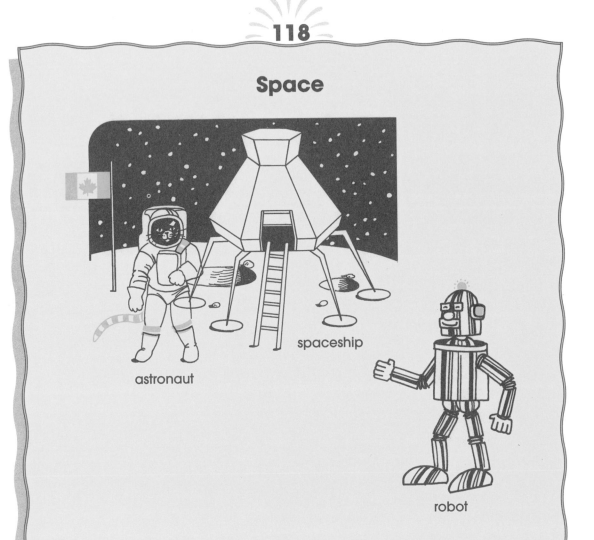

astronaut

spaceship

robot

astronaut	outer	**The Planets**
blastoff	rocket	Earth
capsule	robot	Jupiter
command	satellite	Mars
countdown	shuttle	Mercury
crew	sky	Neptune
flight	solar	Pluto
flying saucer	space arm	Saturn
galaxy, galaxies	space station	Uranus
gravity	spaceship	Venus
launch pad	spacesuit	
lunar	spacewalk	
mission control	starship	
moon	sun	
orbit	touchdown	

Sports

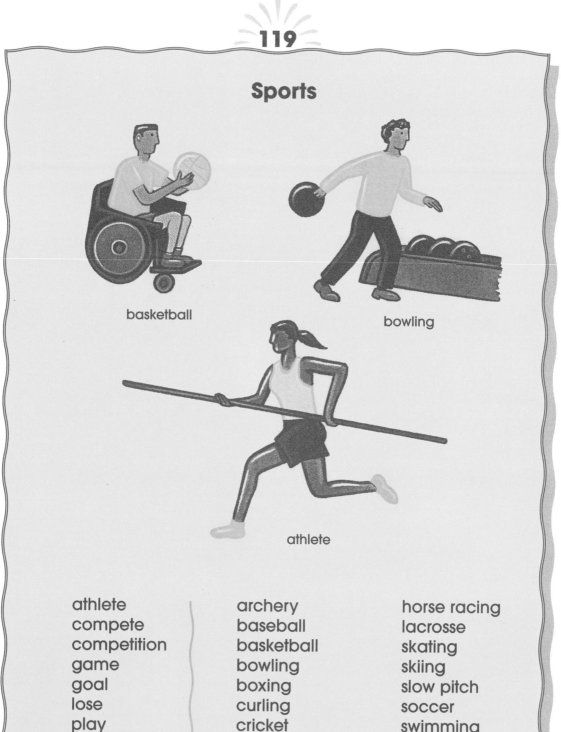

basketball

bowling

athlete

athlete	archery	horse racing
compete	baseball	lacrosse
competition	basketball	skating
game	bowling	skiing
goal	boxing	slow pitch
lose	curling	soccer
play	cricket	swimming
player	diving	tennis
race	figure skating	track and field
score	football	volleyball
team	golf	water skiing
win	gymnastics	wrestling
	hockey	

Transportation

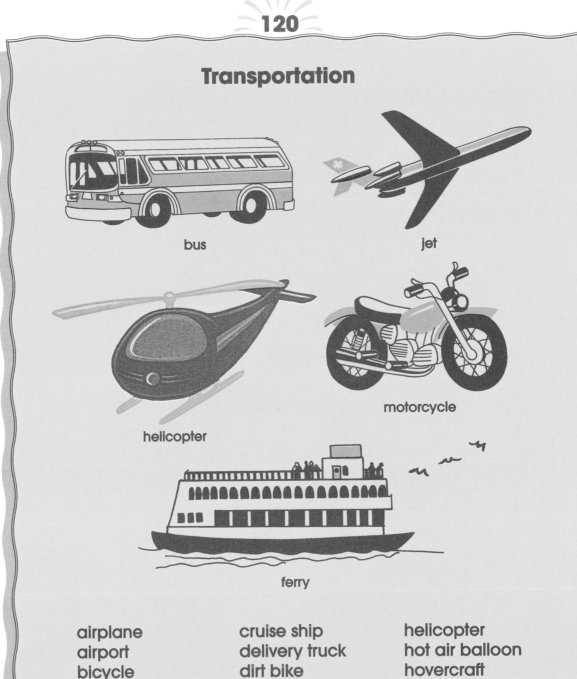

bus

jet

helicopter

motorcycle

ferry

airplane	cruise ship	helicopter
airport	delivery truck	hot air balloon
bicycle	dirt bike	hovercraft
boat	driver	jet
bus	dump truck	journey
camper	engineer	jumbo jet
canoe	ferry	limousine
car	fire engine	motorboat
chopper	flight	motorcycle
coach	freighter	mountain bike
conductor	garbage truck	ocean liner

ship

sailboat

train

truck

passenger
pilot
port
railroad
rowboat
sailboat
seaplane
ship
skateboard
snowmobile

speedboat
station
station wagon
streetcar
submarine
subway
takeoff
taxi
terminal
train

transport
travel, traveller
trip
trolley bus
truck
tugboat
van
yacht

The Weather

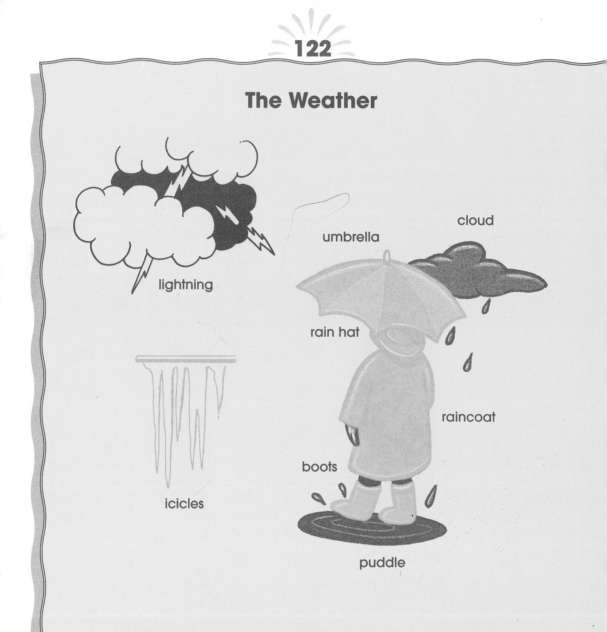

lightning

umbrella

cloud

rain hat

raincoat

boots

icicles

puddle

autumn	fall	humid
avalanche	fluffy	hurricane
blizzard	flurry, flurries	ice
blow	fog	icicle
blustery	forecast	lightning
boots	freeze, freezing	melt
cloud, cloudy	frost	mile
cold	hail	mittens
damp	hailstone	puddle
dark	hot	rain, rainy
drift	howl	rainbow

sunglasses

snowflakes

sun

raincoat	snowfall	thaw
raindrop	snowflake	thermometer
rainfall	snow storm	thunder
rain hat	snowsuit	tornado
rainstorm	spring	twister
satellite	storm	umbrella
scarf	summer	warning
shiver	sun, sunny	wind, windy
sleet	sunglasses	windchill
slush	sun hat	winter
snow, snowy	sunscreen	wintry
snowbank	sunshine	
snow boots	temperature	

Wild Animals

polar bear

walrus

blue jay

cardinal

goose

skunk

In Cold Places
penguin
polar bear
reindeer
seal
walrus

In the Air
bat
blue jay
cardinal
chickadee
goose
gull
hawk

hummingbird
owl
robin
sparrow
woodpecker
wren

**In the Fields
and Forests**
bear
beaver
chipmunk
coyote
deer
elk

fox
frog
groundhog
moose
mouse
porcupine
rabbit
raccoon
skunk
snake
squirrel
toad
weasel
wolf

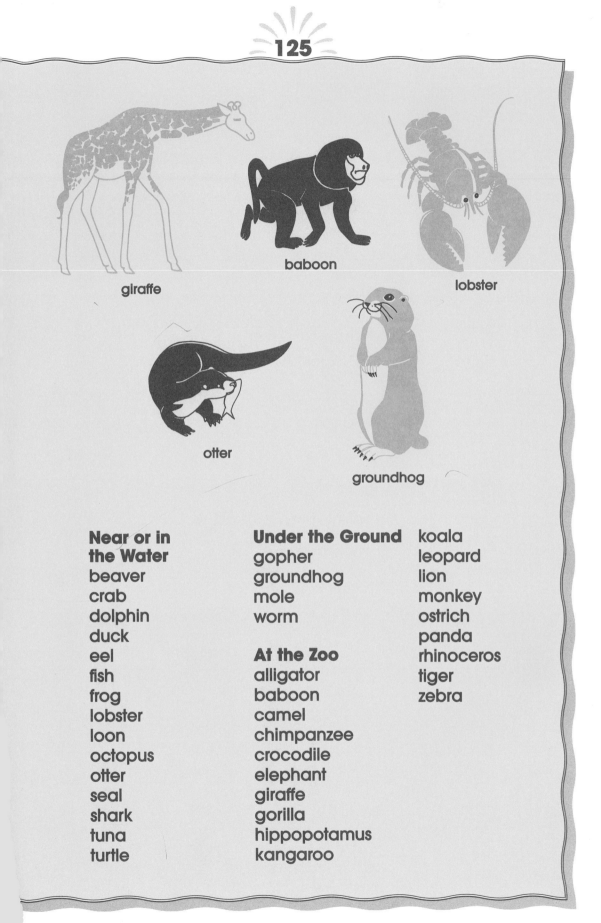

giraffe

baboon

lobster

otter

groundhog

Near or in the Water
beaver
crab
dolphin
duck
eel
fish
frog
lobster
loon
octopus
otter
seal
shark
tuna
turtle

Under the Ground
gopher
groundhog
mole
worm

At the Zoo
alligator
baboon
camel
chimpanzee
crocodile
elephant
giraffe
gorilla
hippopotamus
kangaroo
koala
leopard
lion
monkey
ostrich
panda
rhinoceros
tiger
zebra

Numbers

0	zero				
1	one	11	eleven	30	thirty
2	two	12	twelve	40	forty
3	three	13	thirteen	50	fifty
4	four	14	fourteen	60	sixty
5	five	15	fifteen	70	seventy
6	six	16	sixteen	80	eighty
7	seven	17	seventeen	90	ninety
8	eight	18	eighteen	100	one hundred
9	nine	19	nineteen	1000	one thousand
10	ten	20	twenty	1 000 000	one million

Metric Symbols

cm	centimetre	g	gram	m	metre
kg	kilogram	km	kilometre	mL	millilitre
L	litre				

Days of the Week

Sunday	Sun.
Monday	Mon.
Tuesday	Tues.
Wednesday	Wed.
Thursday	Thurs.
Friday	Fri.
Saturday	Sat.

Months of the Year

January	Jan.
February	Feb.
March	Mar.
April	Apr.
May	May
June	Jun.
July	Jul.
August	Aug.
September	Sept.
October	Oct.
November	Nov.
December	Dec.

Provinces of Canada

British Columbia	B.C.
Alberta	Alta.
Saskatchewan	Sask.
Manitoba	Man.
Ontario	Ont.
Quebec	Que.
New Brunswick	N.B.
Nova Scotia	N.S.
Prince Edward Island	P.E.I.
Newfoundland	Nfld.

Territories

Yukon	Y.T.
Northwest Territories	N.W.T.

The Words We Use Most Often

a	of
all	on
and	one
are	out
at	said
but	she
day	so
for	that
go	the
got	then
had	there
have	they
he	to
his	up
I	was
in	we
is	went
it	were
like	when
me	with
my	you

Printed and bound in Canada

4 5 /BP/98